BRIDGES

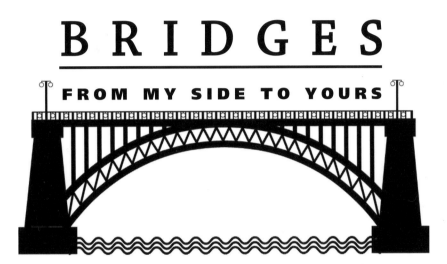

FROM MY SIDE TO YOURS

BRIDGES

From My Side to Yours

Written & Illustrated by Jan Adkins

ROARING BROOK PRESS
BROOKFIELD, CONNECTICUT

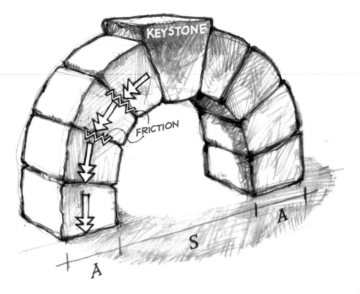

Copyright © 2002 by Jan Adkins,
persistent if nothing else.

Published by Roaring Brook Press, a division of The Millbrook Press,
2 Old New Milford Road, Brookfield, Connecticut 06804.

Library of Congress Cataloging-in-Publication Data
Adkins, Jan.
Bridges : from my side to yours / written & illustrated by Jan Adkins.
        p.cm.
Summary: A look at bridges throughout history, from simple arrangements of stepping stones, to famous landmarks such as London Bridge, to marvels of engineering such as New York's Brooklyn Bridge.
1. Bridges—History—Juvenile literature. [1. Bridges—History.] I. Title.
TG148 .A35 2002
624'.2—dc21   2001048297

ISBN 0-7613-1542-X (trade)
10 9 8 7 6 5 4 3 2 1

ISBN 0-7613-2510-7 (library binding)
10 9 8 7 6 5 4 3 2 1

Printed in the United States of America
First edition

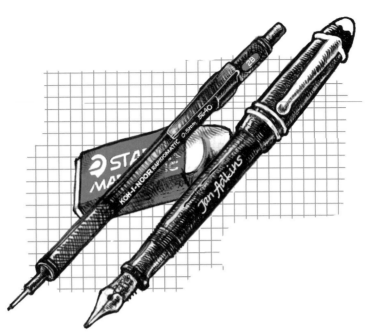

This book could not have been written without friendship and love. The counsel, support, assistance, patience, and benevolent wisdom of Eric DeLony were indispensable. He has been a steady friend since we were students together at Ohio State University. Quiet, unflaggingly polite, but exhibiting occasionally shocking flashes of exuberance, Eric became the director of the Historic American Engineering Record within the National Park Service, recording the heritage of our nation's technical excellence. He chose most of the important bridges in this book and wrote his own superb book, *Landmark American Bridges* (American Society of Civil Engineers, 1993). Eric is an authority on the history of engineering and on the skills of friendship.

Nor could the book have come to you without its editor, Simon Boughton, who has given me faith and trust over a long road. A writer needs a good editor to grow in his work, to keep him honest, and even to retain hope.

Three other friends are constant supports for me: John Swain Carter, my hearty shipmate; John Grandits, the finest art director, typographer, and ex-hippie I know; Spurge, who has shared his studio and everything else with me.

The central pillar of my support and sanity is my daughter, Sally. She has taught me most of what I know about family and love and trust.

Without my family — Sally and my sons, Sam and Web, and my sister Judy — where would I be? How could I write or draw? I am wealthy in love and deeply grateful.

Hell Gate
railroad bridge,
New York City

Contents

Introduction

HIGHWAYS just outside your door connect you to the world. Where could you go? Anywhere: east, west, north, south, traveling fast on wide, smooth roads, across the continent.

From a small bridge over a gentle stream (above) to a modern engineering marvel like the 153-mile (246-kilometer) series of concrete bridges that connects Key West with the Florida mainland (opposite), the history of bridge building is the history of ideas.

You might stop in a traffic jam or at a toll booth. At gas stations, restaurants, motels. You would stop at restrooms all over the country. But to cross the biggest and most difficult obstacles—rivers, streams, gorges—you wouldn't pause. You would ride up and over swift, flowing water . . . on a bridge.

You could travel east to New York City across the mighty Verrazano Narrows Bridge and then across the Brooklyn Bridge. You could travel

south and along the 153-mile (246-kilometer) string of bridges that connects Key West with the Florida mainland. You could travel west and cross the Golden Gate Bridge that connects San Francisco to the Marin Peninsula. Bridges make connections. They make the life on my side of the bridge part of your life.

This book is a kind of bridge to the past. It is a path across a river of ten thousand years to bridge builders of other times and other places.

Nothing has challenged our creativity quite as much or quite so long as bridge building. When we look at a bridge today—even a small bridge over a gentle stream—we see ten thousand years of ideas. Crossing any bridge from my side to yours, we travel with all the head-scratching, late-night-pacing, idea-doodling thinkers and builders that designed bridges—the engineers. Their bridges showed us how to solve problems. Some of their ideas didn't work. Bridges fell down. New ideas are always risky. But every failure taught them something important. Building ideas and making connections is like that.

Stone and Wood

THE FIRST BRIDGES weren't even bridges. You can cross the waters by wading across where the riverbank is firm and the water is shallow over a hard bottom: a ford. Fords were a good way to cross—except when the water rose during floods. Towns grew up at fords. You can see some of them on the map: Bedford, Medford, Rumford, Chadds Ford.

Stepping-stones are simple and useful, in a Japanese garden or across this stream in the Lake District in northwest England (below). They make a scenic crossing in fine weather, but high water, moss, ice, or a struggling lamb might cause a ducking.

Another way of crossing was by boat, a ferry. A ferry could be as small as a rowboat or as large as a steamship. Many river towns were established around ferries: Harpers Ferry, West Virginia; Martins Ferry, Ohio. Ferries are still a practical solution where the water is wide and the traffic is light. Many coastal towns have ferries: the Staten Island Ferry in New York, the Martha's Vineyard and Nantucket ferries in Massachusetts, the Sausalito Ferry to San Francisco, and the Bellhaven Ferry in Seattle.

Ferries have always been important to life on San Francisco Bay. Before the Golden Gate Bridge was built, a trip from San Francisco to Sausalito by land was more than 120 miles (190 kilometers)— if you could cross the Sacramento River. Roads and railroads from northern California stopped at the Sausalito Ferry Terminal, where passengers, cars, mail, and freight were shifted to a steam ferry like the *Saucelito* (below). Today, thousands of commuters still board a ferry (above) for a pleasant 20-minute ride across the bay.

A bridge made from a split tree trunk. According to legend, Robin Hood and Little John tested each other's skill with the quarterstaff on such a bridge.

BUILD A BRIDGE. What will you use? The story of bridges is a story of materials. People have always been clever about using what was available. They have invented new and better ways to use materials, even when their tools were bones and rocks. They did the best work possible with their tools and skills and materials—their *technology*.

Travel back about ten thousand years to the Stone Age, when people were learning to shape and use stone for tools. Their first bridges were accidental—tree trunks fallen across steep stream banks, stepping-stone boulders in creeks. If the people of a village needed to cross the same stream over and over, they might choose a straight tree near the stream and cut it with stone axes. Surely they would notch the trunk so it fell in the direction of the stream. Of course they would cut the branches off. How many villagers would be needed to move the tree trunk—bit by bit —to the best place with tree-branch levers? In an afternoon or a day they might move one end across the stream. Thinking ahead, they might raise both ends on flat boulders to lift it above the spring floods. They might even use wedges to split the log and make a flat walking surface.

A good log bridge might take a few days to finish. The people of the village would decide if crossing the stream easily was worth the work. This is an important bridge fact: Every bridge grows out of people's needs and is built by people's work, whether it is local people cutting tree trunks or local people paying taxes. When you see a bridge you are looking at a community: a tribe or a town or a business.

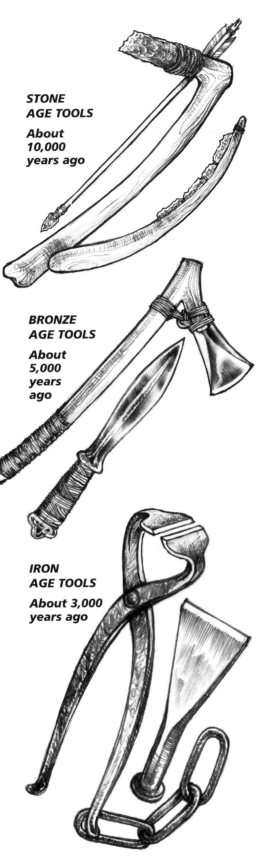

STONE AGE TOOLS

About 10,000 years ago

BRONZE AGE TOOLS

About 5,000 years ago

IRON AGE TOOLS

About 3,000 years ago

The Stone Age, Bronze Age, and Iron Age are levels of toolmaking ability.

The Stone Age civilization worked with flint (stone) axes and obsidian (stone) knives. They used flint arrow-heads to hunt and fire-hardened wooden sticks to plant and hoe.

In the Bronze Age, civilizations (like the early Egyptians) learned to mine and melt soft metals— lead, gold, silver, tin, and copper. They blended tin and copper to make a harder metal, bronze, for sharper and more durable tools and weapons.

In the Iron Age, civilizations (like the Romans) learned to work with very high heat to make iron, a much stronger metal. We can't point to a year and say: This is when everyone started to use iron. Civilizations progress at different rates. There are still isolated groups of people—intelligent, artistic people— who do not use metal. They live in their own Stone Age.

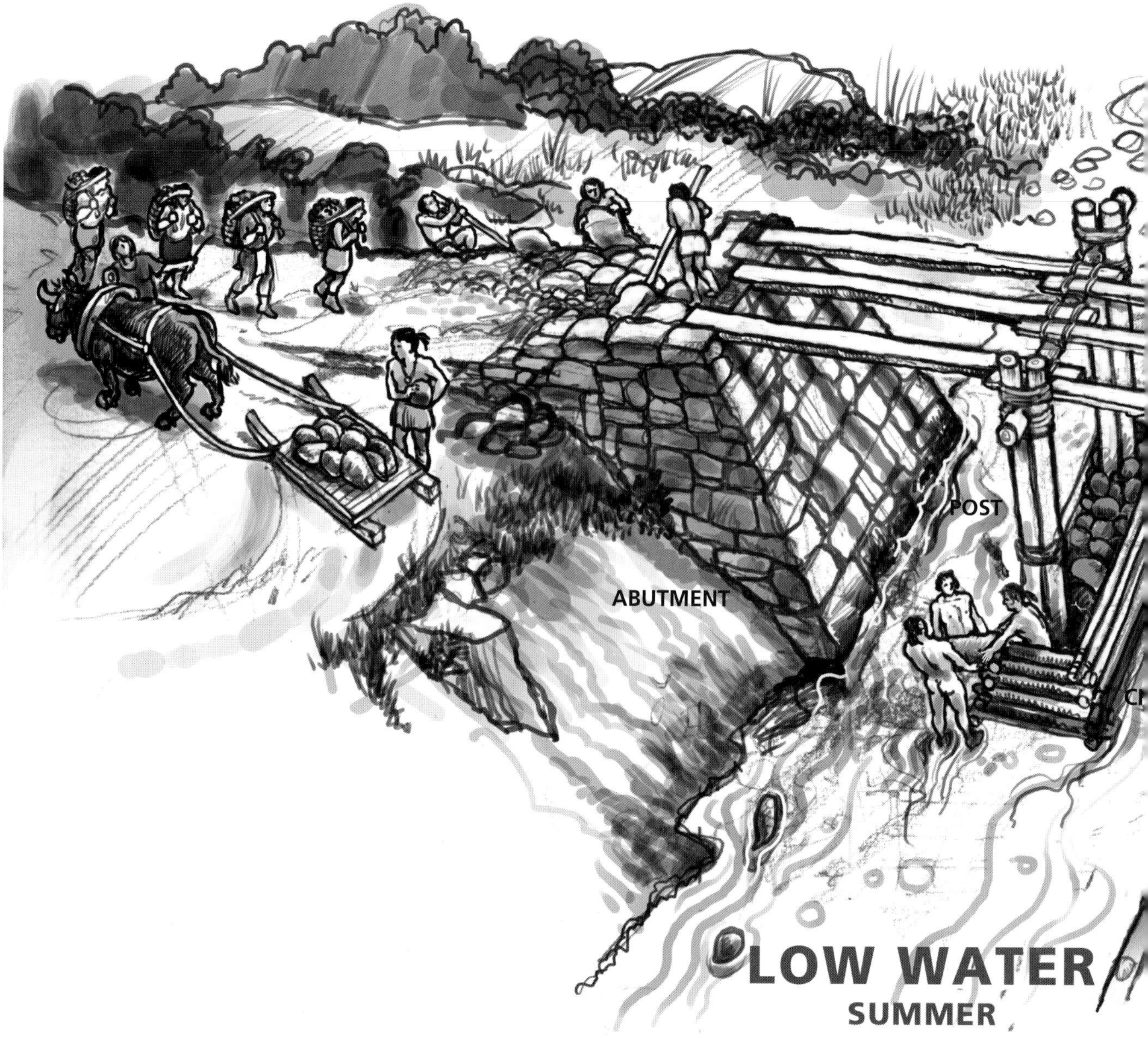

POST

ABUTMENT

LOW WATER
SUMMER

QUESTIONS COME BEFORE BRIDGES. What will cross this bridge? How heavy will the load be? Where is the best place to cross? How swift is the water? How high does the water get? What about ice in the winter? The answers will guide the design of a bridge's structure.

One of the oldest and simplest bridge designs is a post-and-beam structure (above). A bridge like this could have served the small city of Troy three thousand years ago. The Trojans could have used tree trunks or stone pillars for posts, fixed in foundations (secure bases). The distance between posts would be decided by the length of local beams —tree trunks from nearby forests.

The best place to cross would be a

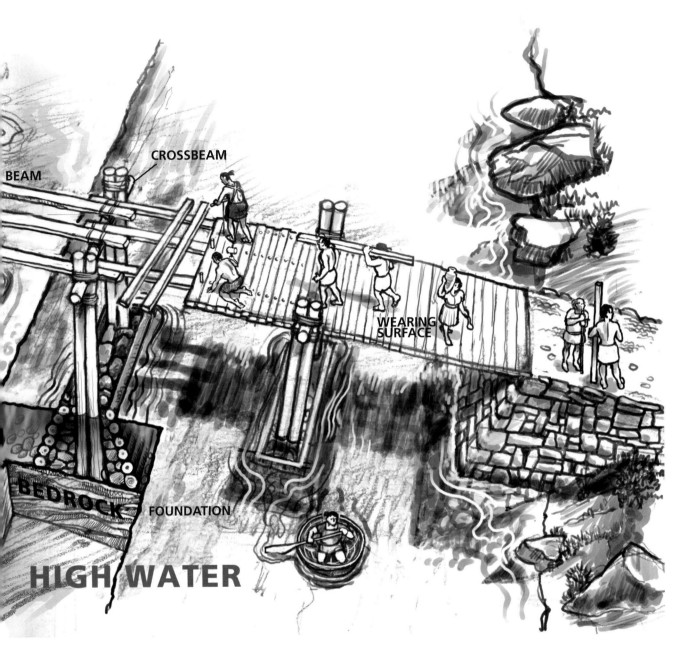

BEAM

CROSSBEAM

WEARING
SURFACE

BEDROCK FOUNDATION

HIGH WATER

site where the banks are steep and firm, and the stream bottom is solid. At summer's lowest water the builders could space cribs—corner notched boxes—of elm (submerged elm doesn't decay) across the stream bottom and fill them with heavy rocks around vertical tree trunk posts. The posts would be connected by crossbeams and strengthened with angled struts. A simple bridge's twin beams would run parallel from one set of posts to the next. Abutments (sloping approaches) of stone and gravel could support the end-beams on both shores. A wearing surface (the "floor" of the bridge) might be made up of squared timber planks attached to the beams with wooden pegs.

Simple post-and-beam bridge at Concord, Massachusetts. In 1775 a force of General Gage's British troops arrived to seize Colonial arms and ammunition. Just beyond the bridge, on Concord's village green, Massachusetts militiamen defended their rights and property, firing the first shots of the American Revolution.

How long could a fine, local bridge like this last? Perhaps a hundred years. But every traveler or cart that passed over it would bend the beams . . . just a little. Over years the pieces would wear and loosen. Water lying between the planks would soak into the wood and cause decay. Insects would eat at the timbers from within. Ice would tear at its base. The current would scour around its foundation. During one of the big storms that come only once every ten or twenty years, or in a spring flood, or in the creaking, snapping breakup of one winter's ice, this fine local bridge, like the walls of Troy, would finally fail.

Local materials can suggest the best bridge. Three thousand years ago some of the farming lands in southwest Britain were richer in stone than in large trees. When people make their furniture and tools and homes with wood and also cook and heat with wood fires, trees become scarce. But plenty of stones cluttered their fields. Some streams were spanned by simple, practical clapper bridges. The word "clapper" comes from an old Saxon word for "laid flat." These were flat, dressed (smoothed) stone slabs between stone posts. Travelers were crossing them when Caesar ruled in Rome.

The Post Bridge is a clapper bridge in the wet, dark country around Dartmoor, England. The posts are laid up of many stones, and the walkway is a single surface of granite slabs, some of them 15 feet (5 meters) long and 6 feet (2 meters) wide.

By the rude bridge that arched the flood,
Their flag to April's breeze unfurled,
Here once the embattled farmers stood
And fired the shot heard round the world.

RALPH WALDO EMERSON,
"Concord Hymn Sung at the Completion
of the Battle Monument" (1837)

The Maine coast is a stone coast. The granite to build Boston, New York, and many other northeastern cities was cut out of Maine's granite islands. In 1928, Maine's chief engineer, Llewellyn Nathaniel Edwards, was asked to connect Bailey Island with the mainland across a tidal inlet. He constructed a spine of granite slabs along a curving ledge of underwater rock, 1,120 feet (341 meters) long. The long granite pieces were stacked up on the rock bottom of the inlet in square cribbing, like a huge building-block set. A wide roadway was built across the top. The open block structure beneath this causeway (raised roadway) allows the tide to run in and out with little interference. Its enormous weight and solid stacked structure stand up against the winter storms. This bridge should last for a while, too.

BRIDGES

Cribbing built of massive stone blocks of granite supports the roadway. The spaces between allow the tide to flow in and out freely.

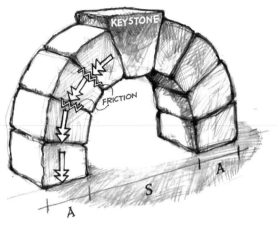

SHAPES CAN BE TOOLS. If you drive a wedge into the end of a log, the log will split. The shape of the wedge redirects the driving force outward.

One of the most useful shape-tools is the arch. The shape of an arch and the way its pieces fit together direct the load above the arch down and out, away from the center. It is a tool for concentrating the weight of a wall or a bridge on either side of an opening. It is also a way to use small, manageable pieces of stone or brick to span a great distance. It can reach across much greater distances than any one-piece wooden beam. Its shape has another advantage: while a greater load on a beam makes it bend more; a greater load on an arch forces its individual pieces together, making it stronger. It is an elegant solution to an engineering problem.

Arches were first used about five thousand years ago along the Euphrates River. Many advanced ancient cultures—the Egyptians, the Maya, and even the Greeks who invented the science of shape, *geometry*—didn't use them. The masters of the arch were the engineers of Rome. They used it to open stone walls and let light into rooms. They used it to span valleys and rivers. The round arch is the trademark of Roman architecture.

Some bridges carry people, horses, carts, and cattle. A bridge that carries water is an *aqueduct*. In A.D. 14 the Roman emperor Agrippa sent engineers to improve the water supply for one of the Roman cities in Gaul (now Nîmes, France). They constructed the Pont du Gard. Arches raise its water channel 150 feet (46 meters) high and carry it almost 800 feet (244 meters) across the river gorge. The Pont du Gard was part of a wonderful system that brought pure water from a spring 35 miles (56 kilometers) away.

Left: An arch cannot support itself until its geometry is complete. A stone arch needs a temporary wooden arch underneath it while the stone pieces are put in place. The temporary arch is called *centering* or *falsework*. Why build a stone arch when you've already built one of wood? Wood won't last. But stone arches built by Roman engineers still stand today, two thousand years after the timber centering was taken away.

Rome, like most great cities, grew beside water. Its bridges across the River Tiber were so important to the city's life that they assumed a religious importance. The *collegium pontifices* (brotherhood of bridge builders) built and repaired bridges. On a feast day in May a great procession led to the *Pons Sublicus,* Rome's sacred timber bridge, first built in 640 B.C., where sacrifices of food and straw "men" were tossed into the Tiber. The festival march was headed by the most important priest in Rome, the *pontifex maximus* (master bridge builder). This chief priesthood was so powerful that the name was later given to Rome's high Christian priest, the pope, who is known as the *pontiff*.

Pope Leo X was born into the powerful de'Medici family and became a cardinal at the age of thirteen. He was elected *pontiff* of Rome in 1513 and put Michelangelo to work as an architect.

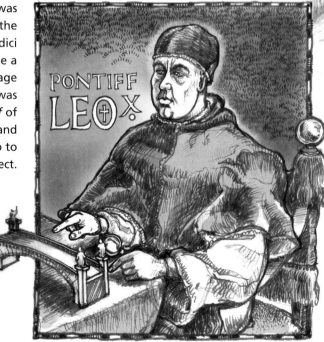

PONTIFF
LEO X

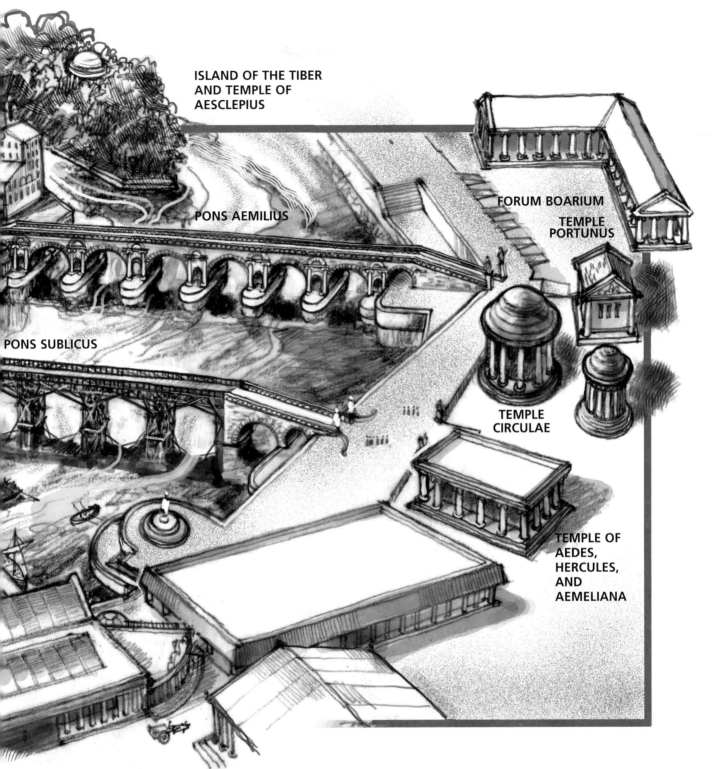

ISLAND OF THE TIBER
AND TEMPLE OF
AESCLEPIUS

PONS AEMILIUS

PONS SUBLICUS

FORUM BOARIUM

TEMPLE
PORTUNUS

TEMPLE
CIRCULAE

TEMPLE OF
AEDES,
HERCULES,
AND
AEMELIANA

Downtown imperial
Rome at the Tiber
River where the city's
sacred bridge, the
Pons Sublicus, crosses.

This symbol of
Rome's heritage was
built and rebuilt
using only wood over
hundreds of years.

From My Side To Yours   23

The Roman Empire grew out of a single city of seven hills on the River Tiber and expanded to embrace the ancient world.

Two thousand years ago you could have walked safely from London to Rome and continued on around the Mediterranean Sea on fine roads. You would cross streams and inlets of the sea on excellent bridges or regular ferries. You needed but two languages—Latin and Greek. You answered to one set of laws—the twelve codes of Rome.

At the center of the empire, Rome was a bustling, corrupt, inventive, artistic, fascinating city with gladitorial games, traffic jams, a police force, and indoor plumbing. Its rule extended from the Scottish wilds of Britain to the eastern shore of the Black Sea in Persia, deep into Egypt, and across the northern coast of Africa. It was the first world power, and its influence on law, art, and government continues to this day.

The Roman Empire's influence on engineering was just as important. Its four great contributions to civilization are tools for every modern engineer:

COFFERDAM

I **COFFERDAMS** are carefully constructed holes in the water. Tree-trunk pilings were driven into the river bottom, close together. Mats of reed and grass were stuffed between the pilings to make the circle nearly watertight. The water inside the circle was bailed out until the river bottom was exposed. Workers could dig into the river bottom below the water's level, pour concrete (see below), and lay stone masonry on it to make foundations for the bridge piers. Romans often preserved foundation stones by painting them with pine pitch or asphalt. Then the cofferdams were filled with stone and gravel up to and above water level. These small islands in the stream, called *starlings*, protected the foundations from ice and floating debris.

II **THE ARCH** was perfected as an architectural tool and used in bridges, temples, monuments, houses, arenas, and public buildings throughout the empire.

III **CONCRETE** was an astounding invention: mud that could be poured into molds and harden into stone! A natural volcanic ash found in the town of Pozzuoli was mixed with lime (heated, powdered limestone), rocks, and sand; when water was added to this *pozzolana,* a chemical reaction began that bonded the ingredients into a solid block, waterproof and durable. For bridge builders, its most

useful property was that it could harden underwater. Poured into molds at the bottom of rivers, it formed a smooth, solid foundation for long-lasting piers. The bridge still standing at Amalfi, Italy, is one of the first concrete bridges. It was built almost entirely of *pozzolana* 1,400 years ago.

IV **THE IDEA OF PUBLIC WORKS** as a necessary part of government and a profitable investment in society was established by the Roman Empire. Rome sent out engineers, armies of skilled construction workers, and costly materials for projects hundreds of miles from Rome. But these investments paid Rome back many times over: Trade moved easily and profitably along the all-weather Roman highways and over its strong arched bridges; city centers of trade and military power were seldom struck by sickness after a supply of pure water was brought in by aqueducts and a sewer system carried waste safely away; letters, orders, supplies, and news traveled quickly to and from the center of the vast Roman Empire.

LATE IN THE FIFTEENTH CENTURY the Pacific coast regions of Peru, Chile, and Ecuador were brought under the power of a great *inca* (king), Pachakuti. His army swept invincible from region to region. They were strong; they had bronze weapons and fine organization. Like the Romans, they did more than merely conquer: They offered the advantages of belonging to a huge, useful family. Four separate lands formed a kingdom almost as large as Europe: *Tawantinsuyu*, meaning "of four parts." Also like the Romans, the Inca linked their empire with roads. Thousands of *chasqui*, relay messengers, ran daily along 14,000 miles of footpath roads, crossing swamps along causeways, ascending mountains on steps cut in stone, following signposts across deserts from one shelter hut to another, and spanning mountain gorges on rope suspension bridges.

Like the Romans, the Inca had a system of public works. Every citizen of *Tawantinsuyu* owed the inca a *m'ita,* a tax of labor. This was not a terrible burden. Building local roads and bridges probably had a fairlike atmosphere with plenty of spicy food and maize beer. Villages today rebuild their bridges every year in the same way, with the same food and drink, using skills passed down over six hundred years. One of the skills is called *ayni*: cooperation in community work. *Ayni* still shapes Andean village life.

As the days for bridge rebuilding approach, each family is responsible for making a certain length of *k'eswa,*

Spider bridges fascinate and humble engineers. As thin as thought, as strong as spirit, suspended by graceful, glittering silk across the breeze. A spider's web—the greatest efficiency from the least material—probably inspired the suspension bridge. Instead of being supported from below, the deck of a suspension bridge is hung ("suspended") from cables anchored on each side of the span. Light and strong, suspension bridges are a practical way to cross a gap that is either too wide or too deep to allow the building of a line of conventional piers or falsework.

a rope of two strands twisted from the dried flower stalks of a mountain grass. When the bridge building time arrives, men twist the *k'eswa* into strong cables about 8 inches (20 centimeters) in diameter. A small line is thrown across the gorge. It is used to pull several thicker lines across. These lines are tied to the spun grass cables, which are heaved across, tightened, and attached to the rock on both sides. Inching out over the mountain gorge (sometimes over a thousand feet deep), a team of rope-weavers ties the three or four lower cables together to form a floor. They will shape and cover this walkway with a basketwork mat of plaited reeds about 3 feet (1 meter) wide. An interlacing pattern of *k'eswa* attaches the upper handrails to the floor. This

forms a slightly reassuring net against slipping through but, more important, it binds the cables together and stiffens the structure.

Building a minor bridge took as little as three days. Bridges across broad chasms, as wide as 135 feet (41 meters) took longer. In 1534, Spanish troops watched Incan soldiers rebuild such a large bridge in twenty days.

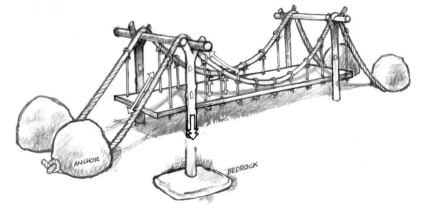

ANCHOR

BEDROCK

After the Caesars

FOR SIX HUNDRED YEARS, the Roman Empire had included Europe, Britain, and large parts of Africa and Asia. Its roads and bridges reached into the provinces, sending out laws, tools, soldiers, and ideas. But the mighty empire grew weak. Perhaps it was too big. Perhaps Roman politics had grown too corrupt. Around A.D. 450 its central power faltered. Europe broke into little kingdoms. We call the next nine hundred years of small, broken states and local squabbles the Middle Ages.

They are sometimes called the Dark Ages because it was a confusing time of battles, famines, and epidemics. Engineering and art were not as important as the struggle to survive, to get tomorrow's meal. Travel through little, warring states was difficult and dangerous; communication was poor; and much of Rome's technology was forgotten. Little kingdoms couldn't afford the empire's vast public works. Old, sturdy bridges built long before the Middle Ages by visiting Roman engineers were far beyond the

abilities of local masons and carpenters. After many generations, those structures seemed miraculous, constructed by superhuman power . . . perhaps even by the devil!

It was a time when spirits of nature seemed closer. Science has shouldered aside myths of faeries and witches and goblins for us, but for our ancestors there was not a dark grove of trees or a deep valley without its own spirit. Streams had spirits, too; some were good, some evil. Some— the Rhine Maidens are one example —were both lovely and treacherous,

like the flow of swift water.

Myths are attempts to explain nature. If travelers drowned at a ford, what kind of myth began? An evil spirit lived there! Most passed over safely, but now and then the stream spirit took someone.

Cultures all over the world shared this myth and an idea that went with it: To build a bridge you must pay a life. A safe bridge would cheat the stream spirit out of its toll of lives. And who was the chief toll collector? The devil. All over Europe there are "Devil's Bridges."

During the Middle Ages in Europe everyone belonged to a kind of stepladder of loyalties that we call the feudal system. It ran from the poorest social class—the low step of society filled by villeins—right up to the king's throne. Almost every person had a fief, a place in the feudal society: a piece of land to farm or a job as a sheriff. A person's fiefdom was a duty he or she owed to folks higher up the stepladder, like paying taxes or serving time as a soldier. It was a social system that fixed people in one town, in one class, and obligated them to endless wars and plots between rival "nobles."

The only large group outside this system was the Roman Catholic Church. The church held great power during that time of sickness, war, lawlessness, and uncertainty.

The church became Europe's bridge builder. Brotherhoods of Franciscan monks believed that part of their duty to God was to care for travelers. They became pontist brothers, bridge builders. These religious brotherhoods built better bridges than local craftsmen because the structure of the church gave monks a good education and opportunities to travel. Because they saw a variety of engineering solutions in their travels, they were better prepared to design difficult structures.

BRIDGES

The bridges built during the Middle Ages copied the round arches, short spans, and heavy piers of earlier Roman structures. There was not much engineering invention in them, but what was happening on them was interesting. Almost every bridge built during the Middle Ages included a chapel. Travelers stopped to pray and to pay—to give thanks and a few coins in payment for safely crossing the water, escaping evil spirits and the devil himself. Even a tiny bridge had a socket on the high point of its arch for a cross and perhaps an alms box into which travelers could drop a coin for the poor. Donations to the bridge chapel also supported the brotherhood and were used for

repairs. Wealthy "nobles" might donate the money for an entire bridge, asking that its chapel be dedicated to prayers for their safety in life and their souls after their death. They suspected that the afterlife might be even worse than the Middle Ages, and constant prayers might be a good investment.

The St. Ives Bridge (left) spans the River Ouse, north of London. Its chapel was consecrated in 1426. But even small bridges might have a cross and a "poor box" for the village church (above).

THE CITY OF LONDON probably grew up around a bridgehead. Julius Caesar's engineers built a fine timber bridge there when his legions were "civilizing" the barbarian Britons in 54 B.C. A succession of similar elm-pile and oak-beam wooden bridges followed Caesar's. In 1176 a priest and builder, Peter of Colechurch, determined to span the unruly River Thames with a bridge that would last.

He began planning the work in the reign of Henry II. Construction was started during the haphazard rule of Richard I, the Lionheart, and continued into the reign of his younger brother John. Colechurch started with cofferdams, then drove elm pilings deep into the river bottom within them. He filled the spaces between the pilings with rock and connected their tops with a grillage of iron-bolted oak. On these

More than a bridge, London Bridge was a bustling street—shops, apartments, taverns, and all manner of city life were supported by Colechurch's massive foundations.

COFFERDAM

STARLING

GRILLAGE

PILINGS

solid underpinnings, he laid a foundation course of squared stone blocks set in pitch. In this careful, massive way, he built 20 piers. To protect the piers, he filled in the diamond-shaped cofferdams to make raised starlings. Between them he constructed 19 pointed arches with 15- to 35-foot (5- to 11-meter) spans, for a total bridge length of 937 feet (286 meters). A lovely river chapel was built on one of the starlings and piers, dedicated to the English saint Thomas à Becket, murdered in 1170, just before the bridge was begun. Beneath it, in a crypt within the starling, Peter of Colechurch was buried. He died in 1209, four years before the bridge span was complete.

The Thames is a powerful tidal river. Its current reverses twice a day, and its level rises and falls by as much as 15 feet (5 meters). The piers and starlings blocked two thirds of the river's width, leaving only 310 feet (95 meters) of water passage, so the bridge's foundation formed a kind of dam. The water level could be backed up above the bridge by as much as 5 feet (2 meters). The rush of water scoured the bottom below the bridge to make a deep pool, an advantage for ships at anchor. The fall of water was also useful for driving waterwheels, which ground oats and, later, pumped water for the London water system. It also created an exciting, dangerous sport, "shooting the bridge," rowing through the arches and down the steep fall of water. Some people, like the seventeenth-century diarist Samuel Pepys, loved the thrill. Conservative souls, like the fat Cardinal Wolsey (1475-1530) and the witty dictionary-maker, Dr. Johnson (1709-1784), left their boats above the bridge, walked downstream, and reboarded after they shot the bridge. The conservatives had logic on their side: Over the years several thousand "shooters" were drowned.

Shooting the bridge, about 1580.

London Bridge became the best address in town. Dozens of shops and homes perched along its sides, projecting far out over the water, pinching the roadway to 12 feet (4 meters) wide and closing above it so that long stretches were like tunnels, with stalls and shops on either side and apartments above.

What was on the bridge? That would depend on when you crossed it. Imagine crossing in the year 1579, during the reign of Queen Elizabeth I.

Entering the bridge from the south side (below left), you pass the Bridge House, filled with bridge repair supplies. At the Staples, stone bollards with iron chains that can close off the bridge, you must give the toll keeper a farthing (a quarter of a penny) during the week, ha'penny (half a penny) on Sunday. The roadway closes around you on all sides, a dark tunnel and very noisy! The waterwheels for grinding grain are rumbling just under you. The folks at The Bear, one of the oldest

taverns in London and only one of many "public houses" on the bridge, don't seem to mind the noise.

When you pass through the portcullis of the Great Stone Gateway (also known as the Traitor's Gate), you might look behind you. Stuck on pikes about 40 feet (12 meters) above—are the heads of men and women executed for treason. In 1579 there are more than thirty heads because Elizabeth is a suspicious queen who has had trouble with plots and conspiracies.

At this opening you can look downriver into the Pool, crowded with workboats and sailing ships. Through their masts you should be able to see the Tower of London, less than half a mile away. This opening has a pillory—a wood-and-iron punishment frame with holes for the hands and heads of criminals to stick through. It's a popular pastime to torment them, but you should move on toward the brightly painted archway ahead and the shops beyond it, selling hats, spurs, needles, food, and tobacco (a strange new import from the Royal Colony of Virginia).

As you break into the light again, Nonesuch House greets you. What a place to live! A "house of apartments" whose wooden timbering was built in Holland and reassembled here with wooden pegs without a nail. At street level the house is mostly windows—small panes of glass joined with lead strips. Each corner is an oriel—a round, projecting cylinder with more windows—and each oriel is capped with a gold-foiled cupola and a gilded weathervane. Flags embroidered with names of the noblemen who live in the apartments flutter on the roof, and shields painted with their symbols hang around the building. Many of

Elizabeth's court favorites live at Nonesuch. The heads of some recent tenants now live on the pikes over Traitor's Gate.

Past Nonesuch House is another long tunnel filled with shops and smells, seventeen shops on the right side, twenty on the left. Food stalls and perfumers, glovers and printers, stationers, goldsmiths, coffee and chocolate houses, horseshoers, candy-makers, silk and cotton merchants. The road is narrow, and you may be backed into a shop door to avoid being run down by handcarts or carriages. The clatter of their iron wheels on the paving and the rush of water below is part of the bridge noise.

A large grocer's shop near the next opening sells good fresh fish. They're caught by the Petermen—the fishermen around the bridge

BRIDGES

(named after the fisherman apostle Simon Peter)—and kept live in a pool dug into the starling.

At the next opening, the Square, you can look down into the rushing water. The damming effect makes it calmer above the bridge, and during a cold winter it freezes deep and hard enough to have fairs and even shops on the ice.

Another long tunnel of shops, sixty-five of them, noisy and cheerful, but you can tell it would be a chancy place late at night. The bridge has its own patrolmen who carry sticks and walk with guard dogs, but there are more than a few robberies. Who could hear a cry for help over the water's roar and the creaking groan of the waterworks wheels turning under this end of the bridge? And bridge residents sleep soundly, accustomed to the noise at all hours, the passing carts and herds of sheep, the gaggles of geese waddling to market, the call of tradesmen, and the bang of crates being loaded and unloaded. Ask anyone in the city; they will tell you it's one of the healthiest places to live. During the plague years only a few bridge dwellers died. There is always a fresh river breeze blowing through the houses above, and the sanitation is easy—wooden jakes (toilets) hang out over the water from the homes, and housewives throw their scraps right into the river. In a few hundred years doctors will learn that plague is carried by rats; no refuse, no rats, no plague.

Crossing in 1579 you would have dodged a lot of carts, your ears would have been ringing with noise, and, by the time you reached the Staples on the north end, you would have seen a lot of life. You might have passed William Shakespeare or the courtier poet Edmund Spenser. Queen Bess herself might have passed under the bridge in one of her ribboned barges filled with musicians playing sweetly. There was nothing so curious or fine as London Bridge, or ever will be again.

In a few hundred years, age and the awful fires of London will, like the bridge keepers in their booths, take their tolls. Weakened arches will fail, and whole houses will tip into the Thames along with their families. By 1760 all the houses will have been removed and the engineer George Dance will rebuild the bridge, widening the roadway and combining two central arches into the Great Arch. But Dance's work will disturb the current's balance, manageable for five hundred years. The bottom eddies will scour away at the pier foundations until Old London Bridge must be demolished and replaced with New London Bridge a few yards downstream.

Even New London Bridge is gone, now, bought and shipped away, stone by stone, to an artificial lake in Arizona.

BRIDGES CONNECT; BRIDGES SEPARATE. Since the march of troops and supplies is the most important problem of war, bridges are the most important and the most abused tools of war. Generals on one side worry about capturing bridges. Generals on the the other side worry about destroying them before the invaders can get across.

In the Middle Ages, before explosives, bridges that might be used for invasion were fortified as heavily as castles, with drawbridges that rose, portcullises (iron gates) that lowered, high walls with crenellations (notches to give archers cover) and loopholes (narrow windows to shoot from).

After the discovery of gunpowder as a tiebreaker, bridges became especially vulnerable. In our time they have been the favorite target for bombs and rockets. More bridges have been destroyed by war than by wear.

In World War II, the race for bridges to cross rivers in Italy, Belgium, France, and Germany was fierce, and the Allied generals were many times disappointed when German sappers (army engineers) blew up the bridges before they could be used to advance. To deprive enemy troops of replacements and supplies, Allied bombers attacked some bridges behind the defending armies. The advancing Allies used prefabricated military bridges to cross those rivers.

Most of these prefab portables were pontoon bridges—a line of boats connected to one another and the riverbank, supporting a roadway. Pontoon bridges today are not much different from the pontoon bridge

The Bailey Bridge is a prefabricated pontoon structure designed to take troops and heavy weapons across rivers and streams.

used by Cyrus the Persian and 500,000 troops to cross the Bosporus in 539 B.C. It was about 1,000 yards (914 meters) long. It was constructed by Mandrocles of Samos, the first bridge builder recorded in history. One hundred and fifty years later, the great-grandson of Cyrus, Xerxes, crossed again with 2 million men (or at least a very large body of men—the old accounts exaggerate), using a double row of 360 anchored ships connected with planks.

It's difficult to see how any medieval army could cross the Pont Valentré Bridge if the people of Cahors, France, objected. Three strong gates kept the enemy out. Loopholes and notched parapets hid archers eager to perforate the invaders. The four small arches above two of the gates are *machicolations*—projecting platforms with holes in the floor. Defenders could pour hot oil down on unwelcome visitors.

Figuring Forces

BY THE LATE FIFTEENTH CENTURY, Europe had become more stable. Little weak kingdoms had been gathered up into larger, stronger kingdoms and alliances. Stability encouraged trade between them. Traders made money—so much money that they began to buy beautiful homes and pay for wonderful paintings. The church was making money, too, and paid painters and sculptors to build and decorate glorious churches. Europe had awoken from the Dark Ages to the Renaissance.

It was a time when people with power and money—like the Medici family and the dangerous Borgias—and creators like Leonardo da Vinci and Michelangelo Buonarroti changed the course of art and architecture. The wealthy wanted to show their wealth, so new buildings—and new bridges—were expected to be more than useful: they must be beautiful! Artists all over Europe reflected a new hopeful spirit in their work; it was human, real, colorful.

Powerful city-states like Rome, Florence, Padua, and Naples began to compete with each other in architectural beauty, like guests at a ball trying to outdo each other in finery. One of the most powerful city-states in the fashion parade was the successful trading port Venice.

PROPOSED BRIDGE FOR

The water-city of Venice was and is a natural fortress: a gathering of small, tightly laced islands shielded from Adriatic storms by the Lido sandbank. Cabbages, wedding parties, coal, and wine—everything traveled the canals by boat, traditionally the Venetian gondola. Every year the *Bucentoro*—the great state barge of the city leaders—led a procession of smaller boats down the central Grand Canal and out toward the sea lanes that brought Venice its enormous wealth. There the doge, the city's chief administrator, cast a wedding ring into the Adriatic, calling "Desponsamus te, mare!" We wed thee, O sea!

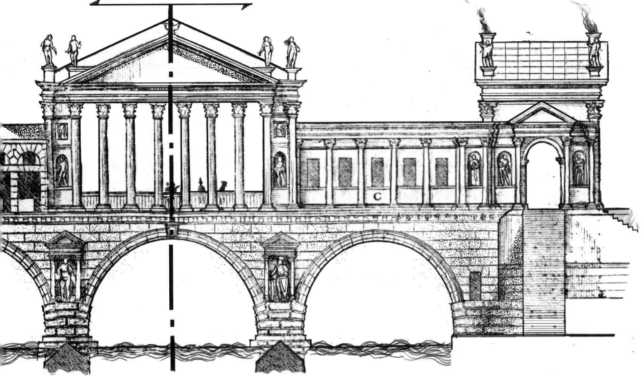

THE RIALTO DISTRICT BY ANDREA PALLADIO C. 1570

In 1587, the best engineer in Venice faced an ocean of problems. Antonio da Ponte, like many architect/engineers of his day, was trained as a sculptor. He was asked to submit plans for a bridge across the Grand Canal, between the silk district and the goldsmithing district of Rialto.

One bridge design (above) had already been submitted by Andrea Palladio, perhaps the best-known architect of his day. Palladio's idea was a high, complicated mess of columns and levels and niches for sculpture. It was a huge structure— so wide that a large part of the Rialto district would have to be torn down, so heavy that it had to be supported by three round arches. No single arch in the design would let the *Bucentoro*, with its long oars, pass under it. Palladio's design was showy and grand and would show up the other city-states, but it was bad engineering. The practical merchants of Venice objected to its cost, to the way it restricted canal traffic, and even to the height of its road surface —tradesmen would be forced to climb long stairs up and then down, carrying their cabbages and wine bottles and coal sacks. It was an advertisement for Palladio more than a connection between the islands of Venice.

The Bridge of Sighs spans a canal between the palace of the doge, the chief magistrate of Venice, and the city's jail. The sadness of the prisoners crossing to judgment gave the bridge its name. The sculptural skill of Da Ponte, its designer, gave this simple passage extraordinary elegance.

Da Ponte was the city's director of public works. He had proven his practical ingenuity in rebuilding the doge's palace after a major fire. He had built fortifications, a saltworks, and a small but famous bridge connecting the prison with the sentencing hall of the palace. Because of the prisoners' sadness, it was known as the Bridge of Sighs. Now Da Ponte was asked to build a practical bridge across the Grand Canal.

The design had to solve many problems. The Grand Canal, about 130 feet (40 meters) wide at the Rialto, is the main "street" of Venice and couldn't be closed while the bridge was being built. The bridge had to be high and wide enough to allow gondolas and other boats to pass under it, but not so high that heavy loads couldn't be carried easily over it. The budget was tight; after rejecting Palladio's monster bridge, Venice was not about to pay one gold piece more than necessary. But of all the problems, the foundation was the most baffling.

All of Venice is built on soft river soil. The only way to make structures steady there is to build on driven pilings. Important buildings crowded close to the site of the bridge. If Da Ponte dug too deeply near them, their pilings would be exposed to air. Then the pilings would rot and the buildings would fall down.

Da Ponte found solutions to all of these problems. He decided on a shallow arch of a single span. This was a daring plan in 1587. Engineers were just beginning to understand that structures were held together by directional forces and not merely by weight. A half-round Roman arch directs the force of the load it carries almost straight down. A flatter arch directs the forces down *and out*. Da Ponte had to build a foundation that would hold the load of the bridge as

COFFERDAM

GRILLAGE

PILINGS

SOFT SILT

it pushed down into the soft soil and would also resist the enormous forces pushing out against the foundations of the nearby buildings.

He began by constructing two cofferdams on either side of the Grand Canal so that traffic could pass between them. When they were pumped out, the canal bottom was exposed, about 25 feet (8 meters) below the surface of the water.

Da Ponte dug three terraces for his piling foundations. The top step was close to the buildings but not deep —6 inches (15 centimeters) above the level of their foundation pilings. The lower terraces stepped down about 3 feet (1 meter) each. He drove six thousand wooden pilings, 6 to 8 inches (15 to 20 centimeters) thick and very close together. The longest pilings were driven into the lower terraces. The upper level, where soil was farther away from the water and firmer, had slightly shorter pilings. He connected the tops of each terrace's pilings with a grillage (a strengthening platform)—three layers of squared timbers clamped together with iron fastenings. The top timbers of the lower terraces went right across as the bottom timbers of the next-highest terrace to bind them together. The result was three giant steps on each side of the canal.

Da Ponte understood that the forces created by the bridge would push down and out in a diagonal thrust, so he laid a slanted brick ramp that filled the big steps of his piling base. The ramp was angled to meet that thrust squarely. He didn't have the mathematical tools that later engineers used to calculate the forces exactly, but he had a sculptor's

sense of balance and direction, and for the Rialto bridge he was close enough. So close that the Rialto has been in daily service for more than four hundred years. Rents from the shops on both sides have paid for Venice's original investment many times over and pay now for the bridge's maintenance. Venice picked the right engineer.

AN AGE OF REASON—that's what historians call the eighteenth century. It was the time of Isaac Newton and Benjamin Franklin, of scientific investigation and the American Revolution! Engineers harnessed the power of steam, experimented with electricity, navigated the globe, and mapped the stars. They also explored forces inside structures, so they could build bigger, stronger, better. Even inside simple beams, they discovered complex forces.

If you stand on a wood beam between two stones it will bend. If three of your friends stand with you it will bend more. If I stand with your friends it will break and we will tumble . . . but how does it break?

There are three kinds of forces in the bending beam. The bottom of the beam is stretching; the wood fibers are in *tension*. The top of the beam is squeezing together; the fibers are in *compression*. At the middle of the beam the two forces are struggling to slip past each other; they are in *shear*. The beam breaks because the tension at the bottom or the compression at the top is stronger than the wood fibers. Or it breaks because the wood fibers are not tightly bound together and shear past each other, starting a rip in the middle.

The Roman arch used geometry to redirect a bridge's load. The triangle has a geometry that makes structures stiff. All other multisided geometric forms—like squares, pentagons, hexagons, octagons—will deform (change shape) if the connections between the straight sides are flexible—but not the triangle. A triangle's shape can be changed only by changing the length of its sides. A connected set of triangles is very stiff (below).

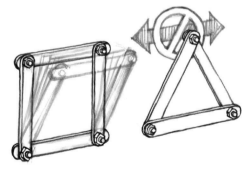

This geometric reasoning gave bridge engineers the truss—a large beam of connected triangles. Pieces on the upper chord (top side) of the

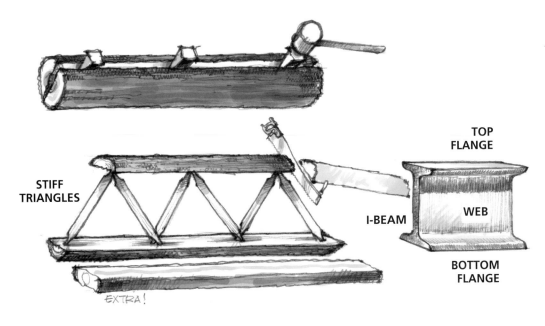

STIFF TRIANGLES

TOP FLANGE

I-BEAM WEB

BOTTOM FLANGE

EXTRA!

Split a log into pieces, then separate the upper (compression) part from the lower (tension) part with stiff, connected triangles. A stronger beam with less wood! The trussed beam is very like an I-beam. The top and bottom flanges are separated by a vertical web. This puts more steel where the compression and tension are concentrated. The distance between the top and bottom chord gives the beam more depth and greater strength.

beam/truss are in compression. Pieces on the lower chord are in tension. Between the upper and lower sides is a web of stiff triangles.

There is another virtue of the truss: It puts the strength where it is needed. Lay an ice-cream-bar stick flat between two erasers and push down (right). It's easy to bend. Now hold it across the gap with its thin edge up and push again. Not so easy. But it's the same stick, the same amount of material resisting your push. Only the geometry is different. A deep beam is stronger; the compression of the top chord is farther from the tension of the bottom chord. Structures like the truss (and the I-beam) put more material at the top and the bottom and reduce the weight between. The result: a stronger beam with less weight.

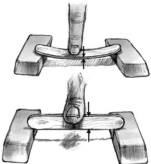

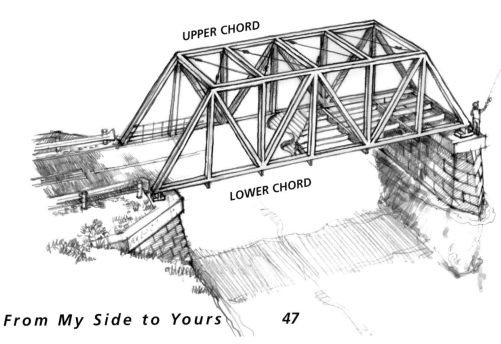

UPPER CHORD

LOWER CHORD

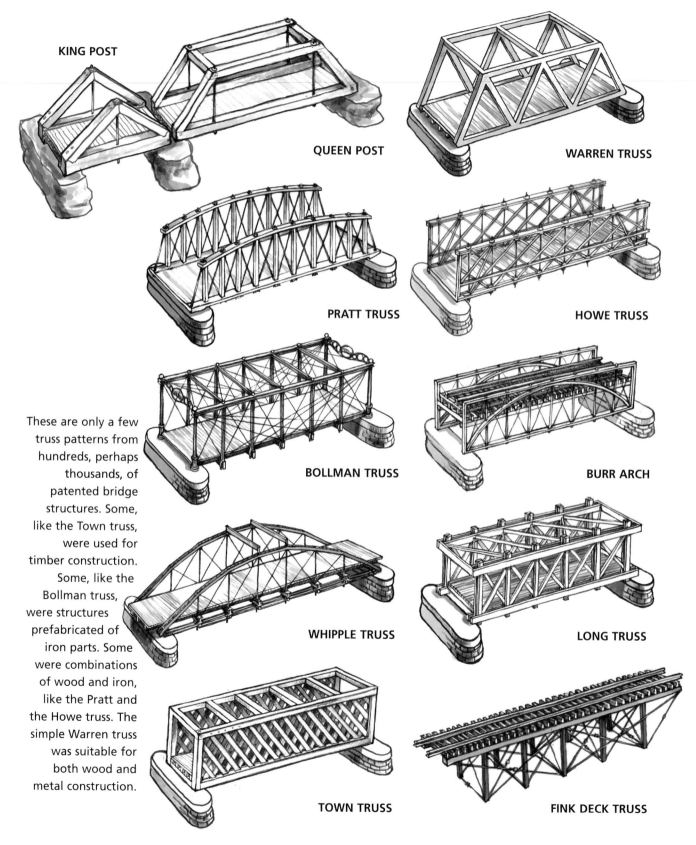

KING POST

QUEEN POST

WARREN TRUSS

PRATT TRUSS

HOWE TRUSS

BOLLMAN TRUSS

BURR ARCH

These are only a few truss patterns from hundreds, perhaps thousands, of patented bridge structures. Some, like the Town truss, were used for timber construction. Some, like the Bollman truss, were structures prefabricated of iron parts. Some were combinations of wood and iron, like the Pratt and the Howe truss. The simple Warren truss was suitable for both wood and metal construction.

WHIPPLE TRUSS

LONG TRUSS

TOWN TRUSS

FINK DECK TRUSS

48

BRIDGES

The arch began as a tool to span great distances with small, manageable pieces of stone. The truss began as a tool to create long, strong, stiff beams with small, manageable pieces of timber. Trusses were very important in a young, rapidly growing country with a wealth of fine timber: America. In the United States, engineers invented and patented dozens of truss types. Thousands of these patent trusses were ordered, precut, from factories that supplied them in many sizes—the original prefabricated structures. Some looked like basketweaving, some combined the truss and the arch. In the big boom of early nineteenth-century railroad building, timber truss railway bridges carried freight and passengers across rivers and streams that had been canoe routes only a hundred years before.

The Red Sucker trestle in Fort Caldwell, Ontario, may look crude compared to a shapely concrete and steel span. But it can support intense use, tremendous weight, and the live stress of fast-moving trains. It was built using timber from native forests. The entire trestle was put together from short pieces and some iron bolts.

Wood is light and strong and easy to shape, but it is vulnerable. Wherever fresh water seeps into its joints and forms puddles, it will decay and lose its strength. One sensible way to discourage wood rot is to build a roof and walls around the bridge's structure—to make a covered bridge. Some covered bridges have lasted more than a hundred years. But they are like the axe that has been in the family for a hundred years: It has had three new handles and two new heads, but it's still cutting wood. A hundred years after it was new, only a few original pieces of the bridge may be left.

A roof and walls protected a covered bridge's wooden truss from weathering and decay. The dim interiors of covered bridges were popular places for "spooning" couples to steal a kiss. This Vermont bridge points out one of the difficulties of a covered bridge: In winter its owners had to bring snow *into* the bridge so sleighs could cross!

Practically, this is an advantage: Worn or broken pieces can be replaced without rebuilding the whole structure.

Early in the nineteenth century, the northern United States was changing at a hectic pace. The big cities were becoming industrial power centers, reaching out to suppliers and markets through a network of canals, better roads, and more bridges. There was a noisy rush of invention and communication, an American awakening. Occasionally, out of just such a stewpot of achievement, a marvel appears. This happened in 1812: The Colossus!

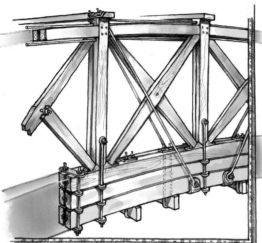

Section of one of the five ribs that supported Wernwag's bridge: light, strong, easy to maintain, and almost rot-proof.

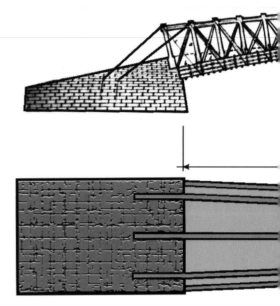

In 1811, bridge and mill builder Lewis Wernwag persuaded a group of investors that tolls from traffic over the Schuylkill River at the Philadelphia Municipal Waterworks would pay for a bridge. He showed them a large model of his proposal: a single, gentle arch that seemed to leap across 300 feet (91 meters) of river like a ballet dancer. No one had ever seen a wooden bridge as large or as beautiful.

Wernwag knew wood inside and out. His bridge was designed to use its virtues—strength, weight, workability—and to discourage its weakness: wood rots where fresh water collects in tight places. He designed his bridge to eliminate tight spaces that could hold water and to encourage air circulation

between all the wooden pieces.

The long arch across the Schuylkill would be formed of five horizontally connected ribs. Each rib was a separate structural system: a laminated (layered) arch with a stiffening truss above it (above left). The arch was laminated—built up— in three layers of strong, light, white pine timber. Each timber was sawn down the middle through the heartwood, to encourage the timber to dry more thoroughly and expose any faults that might be hidden inside the tree. Every part of every rib thus consisted of three pairs of white pine beams, six in all. The layers were shaped to follow the long, river-spanning curve of the arch. Instead of bolting the six pieces together directly, Wernwag clamped them with spacers

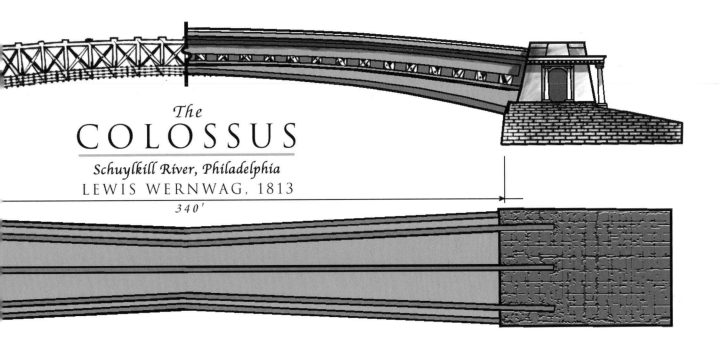

The COLOSSUS

Schuylkill River, Philadelphia
LEWIS WERNWAG, 1813

340'

that allowed air to circulate. He made his timbers decay-proof!

A master of wood construction, Wernwag also understood how to use iron. More than eleven tons of iron clamps and ties and tension rods connected the bridge's wooden parts. Iron fasteners eliminated water-holding mortise-and-tenon joints, sources of decay that weakened other wooden bridges.

The bridge's dead load (the weight of its own structure) was a little over 347 tons. Wernwag considered two kinds of live load (moving forces)—traffic and wind. For the live load of traffic, he estimated that forty to fifty cattle could cross together. To resist wind loads, he angled the sides of the bridge in, so the center was narrower than the ends. Seen from

above, the inward curve formed a horizontal kind of arched beam against storm winds.

One side of the river was firm rock footing. The other side was river silt. Like Da Ponte, Wernwag drove pilings to prepare the silt foundation—599 timbers between 15 and 30 feet (5 and 9 meters) long, driven to bedrock —and connected them with a heavy timber grillage.

The bridge was completed for crossing in January 1813. Its walls and roof were complete by December of that year. Wernwag named it Colossus after the Colossus at Rhodes, one of the wonders of the ancient world. The older Colossus was another waterside structure that was huge, beautiful, and unique in its engineering ingenuity.

In 1821 a hurricane destroyed great parts of Philadelphia. It tore savagely at the Colossus. But the minor damage—some roof and wall sheathing—was quickly repaired. The hurricane proved the Colossus and Lewis Wernwag's creative genius. He had designed a useful engineering sculpture to prevail through terrible winds, to resist time and decay. He had foreseen the need to repair the structure and replace any part. The Colossus should have been

standing still, a monument to reason and grace.

It survived only a few years. It was destroyed by the most vicious enemy of wooden covered bridges: fire. No one knows why arsonists, in 1838, burned the most beautiful bridge in America, strong enough to endure hurricanes, yet so delicately shaped that it had prompted an English visitor to call it "particular light and graceful in its appearance; at a little distance, it looks like a scarf, rounded by the wind, flung over the river."

Iron and Steel

THE INDUSTRIAL REVOLUTION burst the structure of society on both sides of the Atlantic. In less than a hundred years, between the mid-eighteenth and mid-nineteenth centuries, the stable rural economies of Britain, Europe, and America were torn forever. Old social systems changed with them. As painful and destructive as any other revolution, a fireball of industry changed the way men and women saw time, distance, finance, and family.

No one thing made the revolution. It happened quickly, like a sudden storm, because the things and ideas that made it possible came together at about the same time.

In the 1780s in Britain, James Watt was perfecting the steam engine, just as mines began to reach deeper, where they flooded. The steam engine could pump them out. A new system of canals could carry bulky ore and coal from the mines cheaply, and new paved roads could carry new manufactured goods. Factories and mines were employing hundreds of thousands of people. The factory workers were buying manufactured goods and clothes they didn't have time to make themselves. Mills were weaving hundreds of miles of inexpensive cloth. The mills were run by waterwheels or by new steam engines that ran on coal. Everything was linked.

The magic material of the Industrial Revolution was iron. Tools and weapons had been made of iron for almost four thousand years. But smelting iron requires high heat. The only source of such heat was charcoal, produced from small pieces of wood made in small loads. In 1709, the Quaker ironmasters of Coalbrookdale, England, began smelting large batches of iron using *coke*, a kind of charcoal made in vast quantities from coal. Now, iron could be mass produced.

THE BRIDGE AT COA
Designed by THO

There are three important kinds of iron. Cast iron, shaped in molds, is strong and hard in compression but brittle because it is high in carbon. Wrought iron can be forged (beaten) into shape and has a higher strength in tension because of its very low carbon content. Steel is extremely strong and ductile (it can be shaped by drawing it through rollers). Steel is made in a blast furnace that blows oxygen through molten iron; this burns away all but a trace of carbon.

In 1779 the proud iron makers of Coalbrookdale insisted that a new bridge across the Severn River be made of iron. Though chains of wrought iron and fastenings of cast iron had been used on bridges before, this was the first bridge to use iron in compression as the main material. Its engineering was not very inventive—a simple Roman arch—but the strength of iron eliminated the need for thick, heavy structure, and between its two massive abutments the first iron bridge ever built is as light and fanciful as an ink scroll. It has survived intact for more than two hundred years, and the citizens of Coalbrookdale walk across it today, long after the foundry fires that made it were banked. It spans a small stream, but it made a historic crossing from a slower old world to a busy, brutal, soot-black new world.

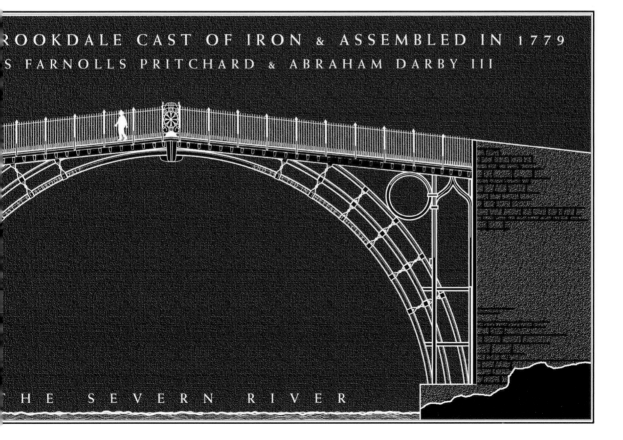

ROOKDALE CAST OF IRON & ASSEMBLED IN 1779
S FARNOLLS PRITCHARD & ABRAHAM DARBY III

THE SEVERN RIVER

IN 1820, THE BRITISH PARLIA-MENT wanted a fast, reliable roadway between London and Holyhead at the western tip of Anglesey Island, the best seaport for a ferry to Ireland. A hard, all-weather, 200-mile (322-kilometer) highway was laid, but it stopped at the Menai Straits, which separate the island of Anglesey from the mainland by a formidable gap of more than 1,000 feet (305 meters). The currents scouring through it were fierce, and the Royal Navy saw the straits as tactically important; no line of bridge piers could hinder big boats

Navy, who had learned to respect the strength of chain at sea. When he retired, he began to experiment with new forms of chain. He bolted

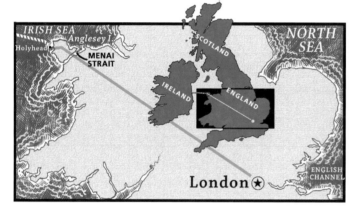

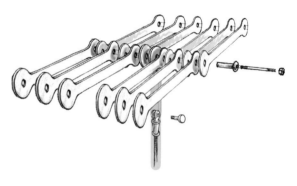

sailing or steaming through the straits.

What kind of bridge could span that immense distance?

The material for the job was wrought iron. Cast iron was brittle and often hid bubbles or fissures that weakened it. A new type of furnace made reliable, low-carbon wrought iron, with three times the strength of cast iron in tension.

The skill for such a bridge was provided by two men. One was Captain Samuel Brown of the Royal

wrought iron bars together through holes in their ends (above). Each "link" could have two, three, or four bars. Using his new form of chain, Brown built a suspension bridge over the River Tweed. The bridge spanned 361 feet (110 meters) and cost £5,000 ($7,500). A stone bridge would have cost £20,000 ($30,000) and taken three times as long to build. Brown proved the principle of the chain suspension bridge.

The other man was Thomas

Telford, a professional engineer who had built harbors, docks, canals, and iron bridges. He and Captain Brown had collaborated on an earlier bridge project that was never built, but the temporary partnership had given Telford valuable new ideas. Telford was given the contract for the Menai Straits bridge, the most daring, most critical project of his life, and he labored furiously over every detail of its design.

In 1819 he supervised the beginning of two gargantuan pylons. Each stone was laid in cement and pinned to the stone beneath it with an iron rod. The abutments marched toward the pylons in great masonry arches. In four years the pylons rose to their height of 153 feet (47 meters) above the straits.

While masons laid and pinned stone, blacksmiths worked at the bars that would form the bridge chains, each 3.5 inches (9 centimeters) square, each placed under enormous tension in a testing machine and struck with a hammer; a faultless ringing "voice" would show that the bar was sound. After testing, each bar was cleaned, heated, steeped in linseed oil, heated again, then painted. Telford was taking no chances.

Telford also took special care with the dead men, the critical anchors that hold the great chains' ends. In a suspension bridge, the load on the roadway is transmitted up through the vertical rods to the curving chain. The load adds to the tension in the chain. Some of the chain's forces are carried down by the towers. A great part of the tension pulls at the ends of the chain on both banks, trying to tear them out toward the center. To resist this awful tension, Telford cut three tunnels through 60 feet (18 meters) of rock on one side of the bridge. At the depth of the tunnels he cut a gallery that connected them. The ends of the chains pulled against connected plates of cast iron spanning this gallery—and against 60 feet of solid rock.

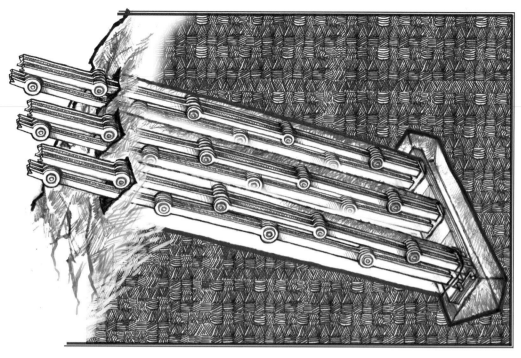

On a breezy April day in 1825, the center portion of the first chain was floated across the Menai Straits on a special barge. The eastern end of the chain was bolted to a length hanging down to water level from the eastern pylon's peak. Lines tied to the western end were led over the tops of the western pylon and back to shore, where a pair of huge horizontal winches, called capstans, were manned by 150 men. At a signal from Telford, a fifer began to screech out a stamp-and-go tune for the men at the capstan bars. The chain began to rise! Higher and higher it went until the tide caught the barge and floated it from under the chain. Thousands of onlookers gasped as the chain fell into the water, but a few minutes later the squealing fife and the straining men pulled the belly of the chain's curve clear. An hour and a half later, the first chain had been hoisted to the pylon top and pinned to its shoreward section. A great celebration broke out. Two workmen were brave enough to scamper across the huge chain, 579 feet (176 meters) from pylon to pylon. Telford collapsed to his knees out of relief.

On January 30, 1826, the Menai Straits bridge was opened. It is still open today. It has been strengthened and refurbished, but if you are going from London to Holyhead you will find the same bridge that Thomas Telford built. It is easy to find Telford, too; he is buried with other heroes of Britain, like Isaac Newton and Winston Churchill, at the London end of Holyhead Highway, in Westminster Abbey.

FAILURE IS A TOOL. Today's failure prevents tomorrow's flaws. The engineering record is pocked by many catastrophes, but each collapse led to new solutions.

Three days after Christmas, 1878, a full gale whipped the waters of the Firth of Tay, Scotland. The wind was rising to almost 80 miles (130 kilometers) per hour in that narrow arm of the stormy North Sea. The Royal Mail train approached the recently completed Firth of Tay Bridge. It was making good time as its locomotive clattered onto the bridge's iron lattice girder trusses. Before the train was a long curve that rose on cast-iron columns to the high trusses over the ship channel, a 2-mile (3-kilometer) crossing over what was then the longest bridge in the world.

Shortly after the bridge had been completed in May of that year, Queen Victoria crossed in her private rail car. She was delighted. The engineer, Thomas Bouch, was close to solving a major problem in British rail travel. Previously, the 45 miles (72 kilometers) between Edinburgh and Dundee took almost four hours. Passengers disembarked at the broad Firth of Forth just north of Edinburgh and boarded a paddlewheel ferry. On the far side they boarded another train for a short run to the Firth of Tay, where a second ferry delayed their trip further. Now that the Firth of Tay bridge was built, a continuous railway to Edinburgh awaited only the completion of Bouch's new suspension bridge across the Firth of Forth. For his contribution to the Empire, the queen had knighted the engineer, Sir Thomas Bouch.

The Royal Mail shot onto the high trusses as a furious blast of wind reached them.

Bouch had consulted Sir George Airy, Astronomer Royal at the Greenwich Naval Observatory, about wind strengths on the Firth. Airy allowed that "for very limited surfaces, and for very limited times, the pressure of the wind does amount to sometimes 40 pounds per square foot, or in Scotland [where the weather is terrible] to probably more." He guessed the wind pressure on the

entire bridge would average about 10 pounds (5 kilograms) per square foot. Airy's low guess led Bouch to assume he could simply ignore the wind. A sailor would have known better.

When the wind blast hit the bridge, the flat-sided train acted like a sail. The sudden, terrific side pressure stressed the bridge in a way it was never designed to resist. The trusses and the columns that held them up twisted and collapsed. The Royal Mail and its eighty passengers plunged, car by car, 90 feet (27 meters) down into the frigid waters of the Firth of Tay. No one survived.

The Board of Trade held a kind of trial, trying to find out why the high trusses had collapsed. They found that Bouch's design had not allowed for wind forces. They found that he had not inspected the materials for size differences or flaws: The high iron columns were bad castings and had holes in them, plugged with beeswax, metal filings, and soot; the truss parts were uneven, which caused stresses to build up in the thinner sections; their connecting bolt-holes were misshapen, causing a loose, weak fit. The Board of Trade determined that Bouch had not supervised the building closely to detect these flaws. He had not inspected or maintained the bridge after its completion, when he might have noticed trouble. Bouch hid himself away after the Board of Trade inquiry. Work on his Firth of Forth Bridge was halted immediately. He died four months later, the last death due to the Tay Bridge collapse.

After the Firth of Tay disaster, engineers were acutely aware of how responsible they must be for their creations. Inspection of materials, building methods, and maintenance improved. And the failure inspired a new kind of bridge.

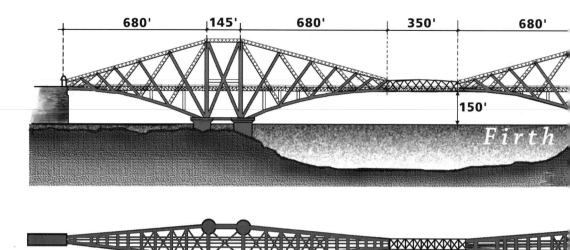

A good bridge wasn't enough. The fall of the Tay Bridge had destroyed confidence in engineering. But the firths still needed bridges, so a structure to cross the deeper, more difficult Firth of Forth needed to be much more than practical: It must be the very image and idea of strength.

The engineers, John Fowler and Benjamin Baker, struggled to present a confident new image, so they avoided any connection with Sir Thomas Bouch or his ideas. They couldn't offer a girder truss bridge like the Tay Bridge. Who would trust it? Trust aside, the Firth of Forth was too deep to build a line of piers. A suspension bridge was out: This had been Bouch's original plan, and in any case travelers weren't yet comfortable with such spidery, delicate structures.

Fowler and Baker proposed a new kind of bridge based on the cantilever—a horizontal surface or structure held at one end. Pull out a kitchen drawer almost as far as it will go; what keeps this cantilever and its load of silverware up? The sides of the drawers are its beams, connected to the drawer runners under the kitchen counter. If an aisle in the kitchen were narrow, mice could bridge the aisle by pushing a drawer from one side and a drawer from the other until they almost touched, then bridging the gap between them with a light frame-work—a breadbasket or a cake rack. Something like this is what Fowler and Baker intended to do to cross the Firth of Forth.

An island, Inchgarvie, lay midstream in the firth at the site they had selected. The cantilevers of their bridge would reach horizontally in two directions from a huge framework tower on Inchgarvie, so that the dead weight of one arm balanced the other. The two-armed cantilever would reach toward a pair of identical double cantilevers near each bank. They would reach but not

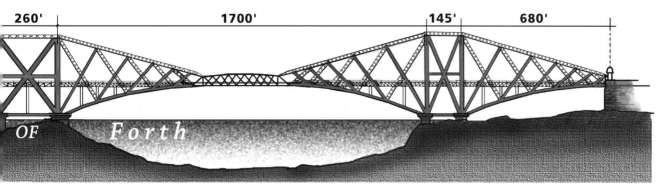

260' 1700' 145' 680'

OF *Forth*

THE FORTH BRIDGE BY JOHN FOWLER AND BENJAMIN BAKER, 1882-1890

This is a demonstration of the cantilever principle for the Firth of Forth Bridge. It reassured railroad investors that the giant bridge would withstand the storms that destroyed the less ambitious Firth of Tay Bridge.

quite touch; the gap would be spanned with a short girder truss. The ends of the bank cantilevers would be approached by a march of stone piers and girder trusses.

Cantilevers had the great advantage of needing no falsework; their parts were assembled outward from the towers. The idea was not new; cantilever bridges had been used a thousand years before in China. The Bavarian engineer Heinrich Gerber had patented a similar construction. Some "Gerber Bridges" spanned more than 400

feet (122 meters). But Fowler and Baker proposed building a bridge on a heroic scale: The distance between Inchgarvie and the shore is more than 1,700 feet (518 meters). Such scale demanded a new material, steel made with the Siemens-Martin open-hearth process, half again as strong as wrought iron. Fowler and Baker would build this first great steel bridge like a ship, using 6.5 million rivets to fasten plates into massive structural cylinders 12 feet (4 meters) in diameter—as broad as the London subway tubes.

Work began in 1882, four years after the Tay Bridge collapse. When the foundations were complete, the steel central towers commenced. Riveting teams heated one-headed pins red hot in portable charcoal furnaces and tossed them with pincers to catchers with metal cone "mitts." The pins were slipped quickly into holes bored in the steel plates. One man "bucked" the head with an iron weight while a hammer man mashed the heat-softened metal into a second head that would tighten even more as it cooled. The bridge rose to a rattling symphony of hammers and steam cranes swinging plates and tubes out over the Firth. It was dangerous work. The skeletal central towers were 361 feet (110 meters) high, and the roadways were 150 feet (46 meters) above the water. The 4,600 workmen were vexed by the Scottish weather—frost, fogs and storms—and 47 died of accidents. A little navy of rowboats constantly scuttling back and forth below the bridge saved a few—eight men—and retrieved more than 8,000 caps, scarves, coats, and gloves from the Firth.

On a cold January day in 1890 the bridge was complete. Each of the three double cantilevers spanned 1,710 feet (521 meters). With their joining girder trusses they made a combined span of 5,350 feet (1,631

meters), with their approaches a length of 8,296 feet (2,529 meters). A North Sea storm was rumbling up the Firth, and it was time to test the bridge. Two trains were run out onto the roadbed, each pulling fifty loaded coal cars with three locomotives at either end, a combined weight of 3,600,000 pounds (1,632,930 kilograms). Baker had predicted that, under load, the bridge would deflect (bend down) as much as 4 inches (10 centimeters) over the length of each

Built massively of huge steel compression tubes and stiff tension trusses, the great bridge leaped across the Firth of Forth from one bank to the tiny island of Inchgarvie, and on to the far bank in two heroic bounds. Three double, balanced cantilevers are connected by two light trusses.

arm; it deflected 3½ inches (9 centimeters). It stood imperturbable, stiff, unmoving through the storm.

But the bridge was not finished. It never will be. It presents 145 acres (59 hectares) of surface to be painted—red on the outside, white inside the tubes—and this is a job that never stops. When painters reach one end of the bridge, the other end needs to be painted again.

The bridge was built in an age of lace and decoration that Mark Twain called "The Gilded Age," whose "artistic" critics often referred to the Firth of Forth Bridge as the ugliest bridge in the world. But if beauty is more than steel-plate deep, then this may be the most beautiful bridge in the world. In 1990, a commission of engineers inspected it and declared that it was the only hundred-year-old bridge that could carry modern express trains at full speed and that it was good for at least another hundred years. Failure built it well.

FOR SOME BRIDGES, spanning the water and carrying great weight isn't enough: they must also move! Building a bridge high enough to allow large vessels to pass under it is sometimes impractical. For many locations the answer is a bridge section that moves aside to let boats and ships pass.

The engineers of these great moving bridges must solve more than the problems of stability and carrying weight; they must also think about pivoting joints, counterweights, and lifting power.

Castle drawbridges were tiny by comparison.

The Siuslaw River Bridge in Oregon, designed by Conde McCullough, raises to let water traffic pass (below). This is usually called a *drawbridge*. There are many ways to solve the problem of how to move the heavy sections of roadway, but most drawbridges use enormous counterweights to balance the load. Both moving sections in this bridge have thousands of pounds of weight on pivoted arms below the bridge's road surface.

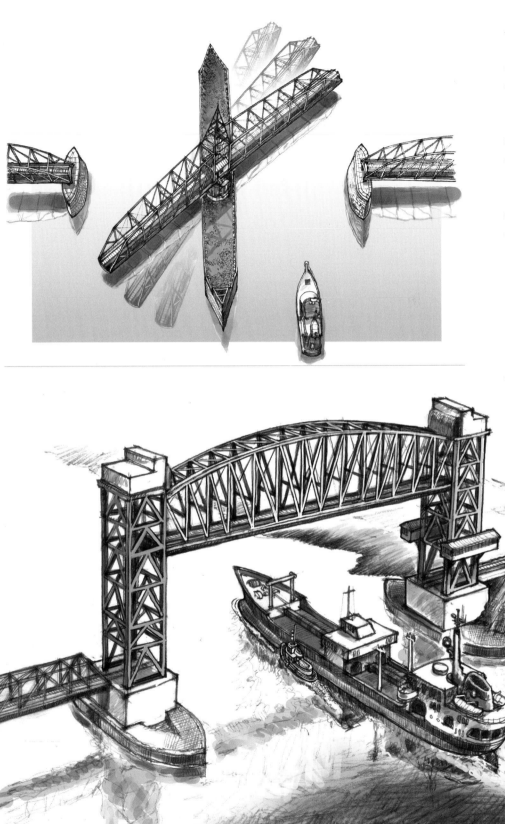

A simple solution for low coastal country is a *swing bridge*. This is a cantilever truss pivoted in the middle. It turns on dozens of steel wheels on a circular track around its center. A motor powers the wheels to swing the span 90 degrees.

Large vessels that need more room to maneuver can pass more easily under a *lift bridge*. The entire truss span is counterweighted and is hoisted up by cables along vertical tracks guiding both ends.

The Big Spans

STRONG MINDS AND STRONG CHARACTER make strong bridges. In the United States, in the last third of the nineteenth century, two strong men were planning massive bridges across dangerous water. Each wrestled with the same deep problem.

Iron cable and iron bridges were John Roebling's business. He was as hard and perhaps as cold as his iron. A tough, opinionated genius, he drove himself and the people around him mercilessly. He was never sick; he attributed his robust health to hot and cold baths and hard work.

JOHN ROEBLING

During the fierce winter of 1866, New York's treacherous East River froze over, immobilizing the ferryboats that were the only link between New York and Brooklyn, which were then separate cities. Businessmen on both sides were finally convinced: John Roebling's plan for a bridge between Brooklyn and Manhattan was essential.

Captain James B. Eads was not an engineer but a master mariner. As a steamboat captain and salvage diver, he knew the powerful currents and shifting mud bottom of the Mississippi River better than any engineer. Commanding, intelligent,

CAPTAIN JAMES B. EADS

decisive, physically powerful, and totally trustworthy, Eads convinced the Illinois & St. Louis Bridge Company that he should design and build the most ambitious railroad bridge of the era, spanning the mighty Mississippi River at St. Louis.

The problem both men faced was mud. The Mississippi River is broad and shallow. Its currents are thick with suspended silt that can build up the bottom or suddenly sweep away, constantly changing the river's course. The East River is not a river at all, but a swift, deep sea-channel between Long Island Sound and the Atlantic, scoured by restless currents that reverse twice a day. At the bottom of both rivers lies deep, soft mud. A bridge's great piers must rest on a solid foundation. How can you dig down to bedrock at the bottom of a river? Both men solved the problem with the same technique, but only one lived to see it done.

John Roebling's design for the Brooklyn Bridge—massive stone towers supporting a suspension bridge— would benefit from a new, cheaper way to make steel, a smelting process developed by Henry Bessemer in England and William Kelly in America. The practical availability of steel allowed both Roebling and Eads to build far beyond anything that had been constructed before. Roebling had

A caisson for the Brooklyn Bridge inches down toward bedrock. Workmen below the air locks, down in the iron-and-timber bottom level, dig and haul river silt by lamp and candlelight. Pumps at the surface pressurize the air to keep the water out. The silt is dumped into water pits. Cranes reach down into the pits and pull silt to the surface in clamshell shovels, dumping it into waste barges. Cranes lift stone blocks into place for masons. Work on the bridge pier goes on as its foundation is being created below.

completed the design by June 1869, when he stood on a piling of the Brooklyn ferry dock, helping to survey the site. He stepped back as an arriving ferry nudged the piling in front of him, but something on the piling—a knot or a spike—crushed the toes of his foot. He was a tough man. He ignored the blood in his boot and continued. Later he collapsed. In three weeks he was dead of tetanus.

Roebling's son and assistant engineer, Colonel Washington Roebling, was asked to continue the work. Unlike his father, he was soft-spoken, modest, and kind. He was a fine engineer and, as his battle experience in the Civil War proved, a fine leader. He had recently returned from Europe, where he had researched a new tool for building on the river bottom: the caisson.

A caisson is a construction submarine designed to go in one direction: down. Both Eads and Roebling used them. A large, watertight iron box was built without a bottom. The box was floated over the bridge pier site and weighted down with the first layers of pier masonry. Once it had sunk to the river's floor, steam engines pumped high pressure air into it. The air forced water out of the box. Workmen climbed down iron tubes to the box's roof and entered through an air lock, where they left the normal air pressure at the surface and entered the high-pressure atmosphere of the caisson on the river bottom. There, they dug away river bottom mud.

WASHINGTON A. ROEBLING

Working in a caisson was strange and dangerous. Wet, hot, and smelly, it was lit with torches and candles that burned quickly and unnaturally bright in the high-pressure air. Pressure intensified noises and made all voices shrill. In this high-oxygen atmosphere, men worked hard but tired quickly. They dug in a constant clammy fog. As they dug, masons at the surface laid more weight of stone on the roof. The caisson's lower edge

MISSISSIPPI RIVER

SILT

BEDROCK

One of the caissons for the Eads Bridge. Once settled on the bedrock, the empty caisson and shafts would be filled, creating a solid foundation for the bridge pier.

cut its way deeper into the ooze. Water pressure outside increased. Air pressure inside the caisson was increased to keep out the water.

About 70 feet (21 meters) down, a mysterious disease struck men in the Mississippi River and East River caissons with sudden, puzzling symptoms. A man might finish his shift feeling fine and climb up through the air lock into the air and the light. A few minutes or a few hours later, he could be struck with terrible pains in his stomach and joints that bent him double. He might simply pitch down dead. Some called it "the bends"; some called it caisson disease.

The cause of caisson disease was not discovered until long after the bridges were complete. Nitrogen gas is about 78 percent of air's volume. Under high pressures, larger quantities of dissolved nitrogen enter the bloodstream through the lungs. When workmen went quickly from high to normal pressure, what happens in suddenly opened cans of soda happened in their bloodstreams: the gas expanded into bubbles. The bubbles caught in joints and lodged in veins, causing terrible pain. Sometimes bubbles blocked blood to the brain; sometimes the heart was deprived.

On December 1, 1870, a fire broke out in the eastern Brooklyn Bridge caisson. It burrowed into the thick overhead timbers with special intensity in the high-pressure atmosphere. Colonel Roebling fought the blaze with his men, going up and down between the surface and the caisson. Late that evening his men carried him, exhausted, through the air lock. On the dock, in the cold air, he seemed to revive, but a sudden and devastating attack of "the bends" paralyzed him.

He recovered, but progress on the foundation was slowed by the fire damage. It was not until May 1872 that the eastern caisson was squarely set on bedrock, a time to celebrate. But Roebling suffered a more serious attack of caisson disease. He was paralyzed and almost died. Again he recovered, but his attacks recurred. He was never completely well again.

On September 11, 1871, the western caisson was towed into place and began its descent. Ten months later it stopped at a depth of 79 feet (24 meters). The foundations were ready. Titanic stone towers began to rise from the East River. Roebling watched the progress through a telescope from his bed on Hicks Street in Brooklyn. His nurse and closest companion was his wife, Emily. For the next eleven years she was also the assistant engineer for the Brooklyn Bridge. Roebling labored in his room over detailed instructions for every phase of the bridge's construction, and Emily conveyed these to the foremen.

EMILY ROEBLING

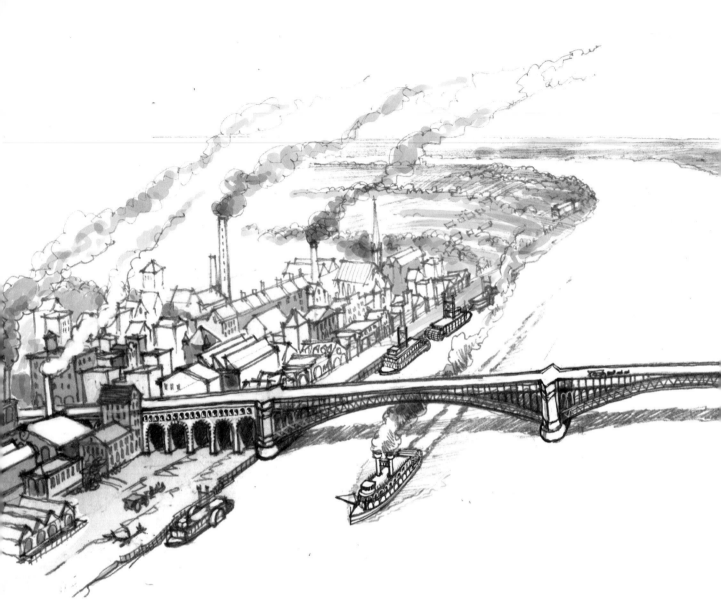

On the Mississippi River, Captain Eads worked fast. His foundation caissons dug through the river ooze to bedrock in 1869, and his four piers were complete by 1873. This would be the largest railroad bridge of its time and the first bridge across the "big" Mississippi, the part below its junction with the Missouri River. Three arches, each more than 500 feet (152 meters) long, would span the stream.

Building falsework for an arch over the Mississippi was out of the question, so Eads devised a temporary cantilever system. On each of the piers he raised a strong tower scaffold (temporary construction platform). He strung cables in opposite directions from each tower. The cables supported the weight of the arch halves on either side as they grew outward. When the arch halves from the piers met each other, the geometry of the arch would hold them above the

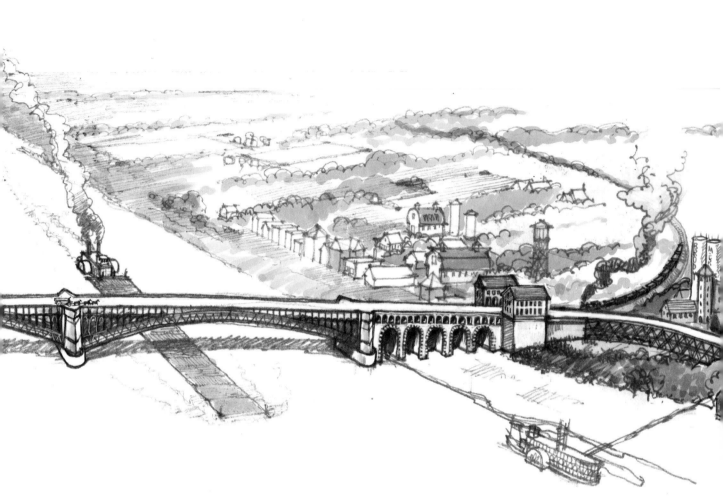

muddy river and the towers could be taken down. Roman engineers would have loved it.

Engineers for the successful Keystone Bridge Company had declared that Eads's design would never support its own weight, much less railroad traffic, and that his method of construction was ridiculous. But under the energetic Captain Eads the work continued swiftly, and the Eads Bridge was complete in 1874, when fourteen Illinois & St. Louis locomotives steamed back and forth across the bridge together for five hours. A few weeks later the great bridge was opened. A 50-foot (15-meter) portrait of Captain James Buchanan Eads hung from the central arch with the legend "The Mississippi—discovered by Marquette, 1673. Spanned by Eads, 1874." The bridge was ready for a rush of freight trains crossing the Mississppi at St. Louis.

Until 1874 the Mississippi River was an obstacle to travel across the continent, passable only by ferry. Eads's bridge was the first permanent crossing.

forces from the suspension cables evenly across the stone structures. The tower tops were the highest vantage point in the cityscape. No building rose near their 276 feet (84 meters). America's busiest cities and most active port spread out around them.

Surely the towers were impressive, but everything about this bridge was on a gargantuan scale. The approaches to the towers, gently rising from street level to a height above ships' masts, were complex structures half a mile long. Built largely of stone, they also included nine major iron girder bridges. Embedded in the approaches were the cable anchors: 23-ton cast-iron plates and iron bar chains held in place by 120 million pounds (54 million kilograms) of granite.

In the summer of 1876, riggers began to "spin" four cables. Each would rise from a Brooklyn anchorage to the east tower's height, then follow a hanging curve across 1,595 feet (486 meters) of space to the west tower and then down to a Manhattan anchorage. Drawn from Bessemer-process steel, each wire was galvanized (electroplated) with zinc to resist the corrosive salt sea air. Two hundred and seventy-eight wires were combined in a single strand. Nineteen strands made up each cable, bound in a continuous wrapping of soft steel

The completed eastern tower of the Brooklyn Bridge, rising 276 feet (84 meters) above the East River—and sinking some 80 feet (24 meters) through water and silt to the bedrock below.

Once the foundations for the Brooklyn Bridge were complete, it took another three years to build the towers. In July 1876, Roebling's men hoisted iron saddles weighing 13 tons apiece to the top of each tower. These caps spread the massive downward wire. Back and forth between the towers, the riggers traveled like two-legged spiders in sliding baskets, spinning 14,000 miles (23,000 kilometers) of wire into the cables.

More than a thousand suspension cables were dropped from the four main cables to hold two roadway decks. The decks were stiffened by deep trusses. Diagonal cables fanned out from the tower tops to connect with vertical suspenders at the trussed deck; the diagonal bracing made the structure even stiffer.

On May 24, 1883, the Brooklyn Bridge was complete. Two roadways rose and passed through its tall gothic arches. Between the roadways two tram shuttles waited to carry passengers. Above the trams was a pedestrian walkway; for a penny, you could walk across the broad, wood-planked promenade and enjoy the best view of both cities. New York and Brooklyn had been united.

Speeches and entertainments went on through the day. Colonel Roebling watched the celebration through binoculars from his bedroom in Brooklyn. In the afternoon a ceremonial party of dignitaries, including the mayors of New York and Brooklyn, the governor of New York State, and the president of the United States, Chester A. Arthur, strode through the east arch to make a symbolic crossing. Roebling had seen enough and lay down for a nap. That evening fourteen tons of

fireworks embroidered the night sky over the greatest sculpture of the modern world, and President Arthur visited Emily and Washington Roebling at their house on Hicks Street.

At midnight, the first moment of May 25, 1884, the Brooklyn Bridge was opened to the public. Over the next two days 313,000 pedestrians crossed. A year later 37,000 people were crossing the bridge every day. In their first year, the trams carried more than 9 million people across the East River. Later that year, "in the interest of the dear public," showman P. T. Barnum took twenty-one elephants across and declared the bridge entirely stable. A hundred years after its opening, the bridge is still strong, still carrying a full load of modern traffic, still necessary.

The Brooklyn Bridge had become a symbol of America's strength, accomplishment, pride, and daring, but by the time it opened, the corporation of St. Louis backers who had built Captain Eads's bridge had gone bankrupt. The bridge was a great structural success—it carries traffic to this day—but the rush of rail travel never came. Captain Eads never built another bridge but concentrated his fine mind and enormous energy on ingenious jetties and levees to keep the mouth of his river, the mighty Mississippi, open to deepwater ships from the Gulf of Mexico.

Like the Firth of Forth Bridge, the Brooklyn Bridge and the Eads Bridge were built during the Gilded Age, when excessive ornament, filigree, and façade were the measures of beauty. But the grand bridge shapes and their stable forms, their mathematical curves, their webs of cables and struts, are all working parts. Their functional beauty confronted the citizens of the Gilded Age with the insignificance of decoration and the robust beauty of engineering—what works.

A New York newspaperman of that Gilded Age, Montgomery Schuyler, admitted that "the work which is likely to be our most durable monument, and to convey some knowledge of us to the most remote posterity, is a work of bare utility; not a shrine, not a fortress, not a palace, but a bridge."

The Brooklyn Bridge

Bookends, two familiar, famous bridges on either side of the continent: on the Atlantic side, the Brooklyn Bridge; on the Pacific side, the Golden Gate Bridge. Each is a symbol of its city.

In 1579, Sir Francis Drake was exploring the long coast of California. He discovered a narrow opening in the coastal ridge, connecting the Pacific Ocean to one of the finest deepwater harbors in the world. In 1846, the trailblazer John Frémont called it "The Golden Gate" to western prosperity. In 1848, real gold was discovered, and a year later get-rich-quick hordes of "forty-niners" crowded through the Gate. By 1900, progressive San Franciscans were looking for a fast way across the Golden Gate to the busy Marin Peninsula to the north.

No bridge had spanned water as broad, deep, and treacherous. San Francisco Bay is enormous, more than 50 miles (80 kilometers) long from the lower bay to the upper reaches of San Pablo Bay. The snow-fed Sacramento River pours in from the north, meeting strong Pacific tides that surge in and out through a slit in the rocks just 4,000 feet (1,220 meters) wide. The currents tearing back and forth through the Golden Gate scour a channel more than 250 feet (76 meters) deep.

So it wasn't until 1918, after the First World War, that San Francisco built up enough trust to ask a local

engineer (and political friend of the city engineer), Joseph B. Strauss, for a feasibility study—could a bridge be built? Strauss was a small man, only 5 feet (1.5 meters) tall, but he had built big things—more than 400 bridges in the United States, Japan, Egypt, and even across the Neva River in Russia. Strauss had patented varieties of drawbridges and had consulted on the drawbridge section of the Arlington Memorial Bridge in Washington, D.C. A bridge was possible, he reported, and he presented the city with sketches of a strange combination bridge—part cantilever, part suspension, entirely ugly, but believable enough to start the fund-raising in 1923.

A small furor erupted. It is difficult for us to think of San Francisco without the great bridge,

but in 1923 it was difficult for a great many San Franciscans to picture the Golden Gate with a nasty bridge. Weren't there enough ferries to Sausalito? Given Strauss's first design, they had a point.

The finest engineers in the country presented proposals and bids for the project. Most estimates ranged from $60 million to $120 million. Joseph Strauss submitted a low bid of $17 million and, in 1929, was named chief engineer. He had never built a suspension bridge, but the simpler structures submitted by his rivals convinced him to change his design. He hired a quiet, hard-working, precise engineer, Charles Alton Ellis, to help him create a grand suspension structure. Ellis burrowed through months of calculations and research to determine the stability of foundation rock on both sides of the Gate, what stresses the suspension cable must carry, what wind loads it would endure. Strauss, wanting to save money, was impatient with Ellis's theoretical work and tried to hurry him. But Ellis knew how crucial his work was. The San Andreas Fault, a focus of California's earthquakes, cuts through the coastal ridge only 6 miles (10 kilometers) from the Gate, and the winds through the Gate can be harsh. Strauss may also have been a little jealous of the glory Ellis could take away from him. Ellis had almost completed a strikingly simple, mathematically pure engineering design in 1931 when Strauss suggested he take a vacation. While Ellis was away, Strauss fired him.

Work on the bridge began in 1932 with the first attempts to build foundations for the towers. A caisson was towed into place, but the wicked currents and unpredictable waves in the Gate tore it away before any work could be done. Caissons were too dangerous. Reverting to older, more stable methods, Strauss built two massive cofferdams of steel plating around the foundation sites. The towers began to rise.

Local architect Irving F. Morrow was hired to design the outward look of the bridge. He created a lasting example of a style called art deco— bold, rhythmic, and sleek. The shape of the towers around the essential structural columns and beams is Morrow's, a shaped skin of aluminum stiffened with repeated angles and channels that give the bridge its strong, jaunty signature and protect the steel structure beneath it. Some wanted to paint the bridge a neutral gray that would fade away, or a grayish green that would blend with the vegetation of Wolf Back Ridge, the series of hills behind the bridge. But Morrow decided to make the bridge a stroke of brave color across the channel. He chose a warm red-orange to harmonize with the reddish exposed rock of the Marin cliffs, a color he called International Orange, as familiar now as the bridge itself. As with the Firth of Forth Bridge (and many others), the job of painting the bridge's 10 million square feet (929,000 square meters) will never stop. Painters start at one end and work for forty-eight months to reach the far side, then start again.

After a floating caisson was destroyed by a storm, it was clear that traditional cofferdams were the only protection against the Golden Gate's rough water and fierce tides. On the north shore, stone-weighted cribs and dikes were built out from the rock cliff. Metal sheathing was driven in around them. Earth and rubble filled in behind the sheathing, and the cofferdam was pumped out to begin the enormous task of pouring the reinforced concrete pier.

NORTH COFFERDAM

CRIBBING

ROCK DYKE

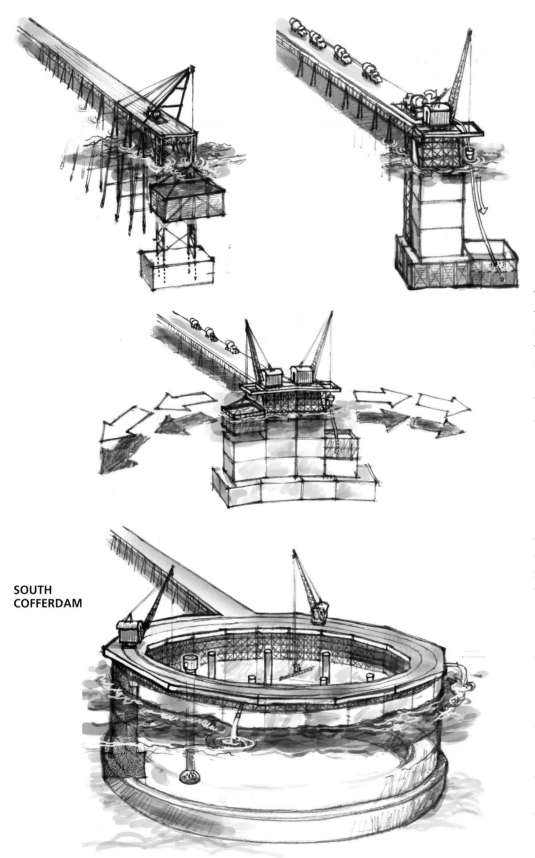

SOUTH COFFERDAM

The south pier of the bridge was located farther from the shore than the north pier and was more exposed to the weather and tides. A long pier was built out on driven pilings. A crane lowered a concrete block-form into place on the bottom. A continuous line of cement trucks shuttled out from the shore, dumping hydraulic concrete (concrete that sets under water) into a flexible tube that piped it into place inside the form. Block by block, the first section of the cofferdam rose above the surface. With its two cranes on a curved track, the cofferdam grew out and around.

BRIDGES

On May 27, 1937, the Golden Gate Bridge was opened in a celebration known as Pedestrian Day. Two hundred thousand San Franciscans and visitors walked across the Golden Gate channel, 220 feet (67 meters) above the current. One hundred thousand tons of steel had gone into the structure and 693,000 cubic yards (530,000 cubic meters) of concrete into the foundations and ramparts. The two cables that suspend the roadway are a finger's width more than 3 feet (91 centimeters) in diameter and were spun from 80,000 miles (128,750 kilometers) of steel wire. The cables' design strength is 160 million pounds (72,600,000 kilograms). The towers rise to 746 feet (227 meters) above the water. The entire length of the bridge, including approaches, is 8,900 feet (2,713 meters), and the clear span between towers is 4,200 feet (1,280 meters). Nothing came close to its scale for many years.

The large crowd of pedestrians on the bridge that first day strained the structure more than any expected vehicle traffic. Celebrating the fiftieth anniversary of its opening, there was a second (certainly the last) Pedestrian Day, held on May 27, 1987. This time 250,000 pedestrians crowded onto the bridge at the same time. The shallow arch of the bridge was flattened, and many engineers feared that it would fail. Currently, there are plans to reinforce this symbol of the West to withstand an earthquake of 8.9 on the Richter scale.

A plaque on the city-side tower identifies engineer Strauss, assistant engineer Clifford E. Paine, architect Morrow, and others who made less important contributions to the bridge, but it makes no mention of Charles Alton Ellis, the designer. Ellis died twelve years after the bridge was completed. He never visited it.

Who should receive credit for the bridge? Ellis? Paine, the assistant who took over Ellis's job? Certainly—but it was Strauss who risked his reputation and destroyed his own health in pursuit of a daring project. He invested ten years in raising interest for the idea of a bridge and worked as ceaselessly as Washington Roebling had on the Brooklyn Bridge. Like Roebling, he was crushed by the work. He suffered a complete physical breakdown just after work on the bridge was begun but returned to the project. He saw the bridge complete and died within the year—eleven years before Ellis. Ellis produced a fine body of engineering calculations and drawings for the bridge. Strauss made the bridge a political possibility, helped raise the money, began the work, and drove the project to its conclusion; he gave it everything.

Compression and Tension

THE CROOKED, CURIOUS PATH from flowerpots to concrete bridges is not so unusual. There are few straight lines in the history of discovery.

Concrete is a lost and found material. It was essential for Roman engineers once they had discovered the natural cement, pozzolana. But after the Roman Empire faded away, the use of concrete was lost for more than a thousand years. It was not until the sixteenth century that a pocket of similar cement was discovered in England. Pourable stone! What builder wouldn't use it?

Natural deposits of cement were uncommon. In 1824, Joseph Aspdin, an Englishman, discovered that cement could be made by burning limestone and clay together. He called the result Portland cement, after a stone found near his home. This stove-top experiment, producing a few pounds of product, was of no use to engineers and builders until 1875, when David O. Saylor used big furnaces in Copely, Pennsylvania, to produce construction cement in large quantities.

Concrete became, again, a practical substitute for stone. It makes good foundations, fills spaces, and is very strong in compression. But concrete is so weak in tension that even a short beam will crack and fail. It can be used as a protective wall facing; some of the Erie Canal's bulwarks (strong walls), built in the early 1800s, are concrete. It was often poured into forms to make modest Roman arches, where its strength in compression was useful.

In the 1860s a French gardener, R. Jean Monier, was producing big flowerpots for decorative shrubs and trees by molding concrete around a core of iron mesh. The combination was strong and durable. The iron withstood the outward pressure of the damp potting soil (tension); the concrete protected the iron against the damp. It was also discovered that concrete and steel expanded or contracted with hot or cold almost identically, so temperature would not destroy their bond. Like peanut butter and jelly or cookies and milk, iron and concrete were a natural combination — reinforced concrete.

There is a difference between *cement* and *concrete*. *Cement* is the chemically active bonding powder — the stone glue — found in natural deposits or made of fired clay and limestone. Concrete is the structural mixture of cement, water (which activates the cement), sand, and aggregate, usually small stones.

cement

sand   water

CONCRETE

Aggregate (stones)

Early reinforced concrete was more reinforcement than concrete. The light concrete coating wasn't really sharing the load with the heavy iron or steel beams inside. It was acting as thick paint.

The oldest reinforced concrete bridge in the United States is in San Francisco—dwarfed by the Golden Gate Bridge, only a few hundred yards away. It is a concrete arch reinforced with twisted iron rods only 20 feet (6 meters) across, a decorative bridge using the plastic nature of concrete to shape artificial stalagmites. Cute but unimpressive.

Alvord Lake Bridge in Golden Gate Park, San Francisco, is the oldest reinforced concrete bridge in the United States. Tiny and quaint, it spans only 20 feet (6 meters).

From My Side to Yours   **87**

Reinforced concrete had practical advantages for engineers. Most of its ingredients were local—sand, gravel, cement—and simple forms could be built by local workers. Concrete construction was good politics, then, because a large part of the construction costs stayed in the community.

It also had design advantages. A concrete-encased beam was thicker. It had bigger, more impressive proportions. Reinforced concrete made a solid, impressive bridge for highly visible or even ceremonial locations, like the Memorial Bridge in Washington, D.C. (above). Built in 1900, it spans the Potomac River between the Lincoln Memorial and Arlington National Cemetery, continuing the broad concourse that starts at the Capitol. It is a powerful, graceful bridge that may last for many hundreds of years,

but it suggests one of reinforced concrete's flaws—it put designers to sleep. Strong and economical, impressively heavy, concrete was used without imagination, often (as in the Memorial Bridge) simulating stone. In fact, it was sometimes hidden behind a thin layer of real stone. Concrete hadn't achieved its full potential.

But at a single stroke the Roman engineer's standby was about to overcome its place as the poor relation of stone to become the most important structural material of the twentieth century. At the beginning of the twentieth century, French engineer Eugene Freysinnet designed forms for concrete beams that enclosed ridged steel rods running lengthwise. Before he poured the concrete, he used powerful machines that stretched the steel to enormous tension. When

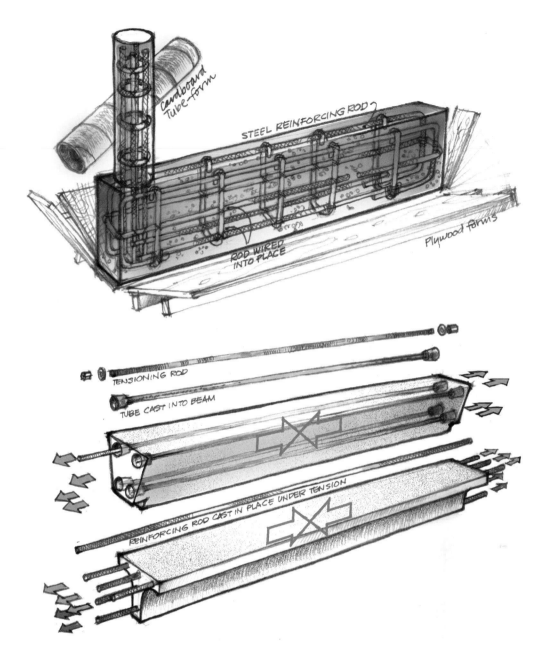

Cardboard Tube-Form

STEEL REINFORCING ROD

ROD WIRED INTO PLACE

Plywood forms

TENSIONING ROD

TUBE CAST INTO BEAM

REINFORCING ROD CAST IN PLACE UNDER TENSION

REINFORCED CONCRETE is simply concrete poured around a steel reinforcing bar bent to shape and held lightly together with welds or wire ties. It is a strong and durable construction method for walls and foundations. It is a fine material for bridges, too, though it cracks and fails easily under tension or bending stresses.

STRESSED CONCRETE creates a much stiffer beam or girder. One method is to stretch the reinforcing bar and cast concrete around it, then release the tension. Another is to cast tubes into the concrete. After the concrete cures, threaded rods slipped into the tubes are tightened. Both methods put the steel in tension and the concrete in compression.

the beam was poured and the concrete had set, he released the tension. Concrete is strongest under compression; the embedded rods and their ridges placed the concrete under constant compression. Freysinnet had created a strong, light concrete girder. Prestressed concrete girders could be made in factories by low-skilled labor and shipped to a building site. Prefabricating construction (manufacturing the pieces beforehand) meant that bridges and buildings were completed faster, and this meant more savings. The steel/concrete combination retained its original virtues, long life and low maintenance—with a big boost in strength.

This miraculous construction material split twentieth-century engineering into two paths: brilliance and boredom. You can see the brilliance in the bridges designed by American engineer Conde McCullough. The bond between beauty and function is especially strong in his Caveman Bridge across the Rogue River in Grants Pass, Oregon (above). Italian engineer/artist Riccardo Morandi's prefabricated bridge in prestressed concrete spans the Columbia River in British Columbia (below).

Its form may remind you that another Italian engineer, Da Ponte of the Rialto Bridge, was both a sculptor and an engineer.

You need not look far for the boredom. Take a ride on the Interstate Highway System and see the practical, useful, uninspired bridges that carry and cross it— prestressed concrete beams used as simply as the log beam bridges that Stone Age villagers felled across brooks. Still, everything can't be brilliant. Engineers prefer practical, and clients prefer cheap.

Robert Maillart's reinforced concrete bridge spans a frightening gorge in a single 295-foot (90-meter) leap in Switzerland. Light and airy, it seems to grow out of the rocky cliffs and meet in a stylized midair handshake. It is a sculpture that carries produce, milk trucks, school buses, tourists. It was built on an ingenious cantilevered complication of centering almost as beautiful—though not nearly as simple and pure—as the bridge itself. The bridge is even more impressive when we learn that it was built more than 70 years ago, in 1930.

The Shima-Marayuma Bridge passes over an inlet of Ago bay in the Ise-Shima National Park southwest of Tokyo, Japan. As light and airy as the bridge may look, it was built to withstand the serious earthquakes common in this part of Japan.

NEW MATERIALS MAKE NEW BRIDGES. Strong, rust-resistant cables, new connectors, and new designs for stressed concrete beams have allowed engineers to design astonishing bridges. Cable-stayed bridges are feather-thin and seem to float over the water. They look simple, but we know that is an illusion. Simplicity is a result of long planning and complex calculations. Computer modeling—constructing a virtual mathematical bridge in three dimensions—allows engineers to pare designs down to bare essentials.

Engineering plans are being drawn right now that will astound all of us. Human ingenuity and the wonderful human desire to push the limits will take us all to unexpected places.

What about a bridge across the Bering Strait? The diminutive builder of the Golden Gate Bridge,

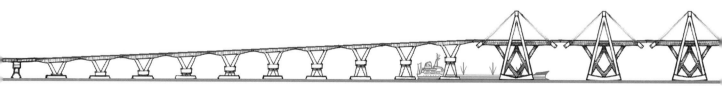

Joseph Strauss, did his engineering degree thesis on such a bridge in the late 1800s, and the idea has even more merit today. It would be a gateway to the natural riches of Siberia.

What about bridges that go under the water? Work is being done on a vacuum tube to be held in place by cables anchored to the sea-floor, 100 feet (30 meters) beneath the stormy surface, carrying supersonic trains suspended and propelled by magnetic panels (above right). In a "bridge" like this you could cross the Atlantic in less than three hours.

What kinds of bridges will you cross in a few years? Is an orbiting space station a kind of bridge to the planets and the stars?

Bridges go from one place to another. Sometimes from one time to another. They represent our cleverest ideas and demand our best materials. They are opportunities for grace, for practicality . . . even for failure. They connect us.

The Lake Maracaibo Bridge in Venezuela (below) spans the mouth of a deepwater inlet of the Caribbean Sea, using prestressed concrete cantilever beams cast in place from a floating concrete-mixing factory. Six high trestles at the center are stiffened with cable stays. The bridge descends from the high A-frame, cable-stayed trestles to shorter and shorter X-frame supports and down to simple H-frame pilings. Each of the central cantilevers spans 780 feet (238 meters). The total length of this mighty bridge is 5 miles (8 kilometers).

Glossary

Abutment   The structure at each end of a bridge that supports its main span.

Anchor   In a suspension bridge, the point at which the cables are fixed to the ground.

Arch   A curved structure that spans an opening and supports weight.

Beam   A long, rigid piece of wood, metal, or other material. In a simple bridge, horizontal beams may be supported by vertical posts to form short spans.

Caisson   A watertight chamber or box used to enable workers to work underwater — for example, digging bridge foundations on a river bottom. High-pressure air is pumped into a caisson to keep water out.

Cantilever   A rigid beam or other structure with one fixed end and the other end extending into space. A cantilever bridge may be made of two such structures, one extending from each bank, connected in the middle.

Causeway   A raised road over a body of water.

Centering   See *Falsework*.

Clapper   Flat dressed stone. A clapper bridge is a series of such stones supported by posts made of similar flat stones.

Cofferdam   A temporary enclosure that enables work to be done on a river or sea bottom. After an enclosed dam is built, water is pumped out to expose the river or sea bottom.

Cribbing   A wall or lining made of closely spaced timbers. In bridge-building, cribbing might be used to protect posts or foundations.

Deck   The roadway or surface of a bridge.

Falsework   A temporary structure used to support the pieces of an arch while it is being built. The falsework is removed when the arch is complete.

Floor   See *Deck*.

Foundation   The base on which a bridge's posts, towers, or other structures rests.

Girder   A large beam.

Grillage   A frame, or grille, made of interlocking timbers, used for spreading a heavy load over a large area.

Keystone   A wedge-shaped stone at the top of an arch that holds the other pieces in place.

Load   The weight a bridge must support. **Dead load** is the fixed, unmoving weight of the bridge itself. **Live load** is the weight of the traffic that moves across the bridge.

Parapet   The wall along the edge of a bridge.

Pier   Vertical supports for the ends of a bridge's spans.

Pile   A log, post, or beam hammered into the ground to form part of a foundation or wall. Several piles together are called pilings.

Pontoon   A boat or float used to support a bridge.

Post   An upright piece of timber or other material. See also *Beam*.

Pylons   Tall towers at each end of a bridge. Pylons may support the cables in a suspension bridge.

Span   The distance between two supporting points (such as piers or abutments) in a bridge, or the structure that stretches between those two supporting points. A bridge may have one span, or many spans.

Starling   A small island, sometimes made by filling in a cofferdam, that protects the foundation of a bridge's piers.

Suspension bridge   A bridge having a deck that hangs from cables.

Trestle   A bridge consisting of many short beams supported by A-shaped or triangular frames.

Truss   A girder or beam made of a series of interlocking triangles.

Wearing Surface   See *Deck*.

Index

Page numbers in italics refer to illustrations.